About This Resource

Why is this topic important?

The capacity of the Internet to transform training materials into exciting, meaningful, and active learning experiences is in many ways only bound by the imaginations of online instructors and trainers. Today's online technologies can be used to immerse learners in cooperative projects, create learning communities, animate complex concepts, facilitate e-learning activities, involve learners in purposeful discussions, and offer learners an interactive online classroom that is a practical and effective alternative to traditional training environments.

What can you achieve with this book?

For most of us, the e-learning classroom is a new environment that requires a variety of technology skills and communications strategies that are not the same as those we have used in our previous traditional classroom experiences. As a result, oftentimes we fail to remember that the online classroom can also be a creative, rewarding, and interactive environment for learners. As a guide when you are designing and developing online courses, this book can unleash imaginative and resourceful ideas for hundreds of online activities and games that you can use in most any online course to accomplish a variety of learning objectives. These activities can be used to improve the substance of interactions in your e-learning courses, and they can also improve learner performance through the use of active learning.

How is this resource organized?

Much like a cookbook, the seventy-five e-learning activities included in this book are written as stand-alone recipes for both your success as an online instructor and the success of your students as e-learners. While the activities are grouped into five general sections (introductions and icebreakers, e-learning skills, collaboration and team building, elaborating on course content, and increasing interactivity), many of them can be used independently or in tandem throughout an online course. In the book's introduction is a matrix of the activities that can also be used to determine which are most appropriate for accomplishing your learning objectives, depending on the number of learners in your course, the technology available to learners, and the amount of time you want learners to dedicate to energetic participation in the activity.

In addition, the book includes more than eighty practical tips and suggestions for increasing the interactivity in your online courses, a glossary of essential e-learning terms, and a list of useful online and text resources for instructors and trainers who want to create interactive training experiences.

About Pfeiffer

Pfeiffer serves the professional development and hands-on resource needs of training and human resource practitioners and gives them products to do their jobs better. We deliver proven ideas and solutions from experts in HR development and HR management, and we offer effective and customizable tools to improve workplace performance. From novice to seasoned professional, Pfeiffer is the source you can trust to make yourself and your organization more successful.

Essential Knowledge Pfeiffer produces insightful, practical, and comprehensive materials on topics that matter the most to training and HR professionals. Our Essential Knowledge resources translate the expertise of seasoned professionals into practical, how-to guidance on critical workplace issues and problems. These resources are supported by case studies, worksheets, and job aids and are frequently supplemented with CD-ROMs, websites, and other means of making the content easier to read, understand, and use.

Essential Tools Pfeiffer's Essential Tools resources save time and expense by offering proven, ready-to-use materials—including exercises, activities, games, instruments, and assessments—for use during a training or team-learning event. These resources are frequently offered in looseleaf or CD-ROM format to facilitate copying and customization of the material.

Pfeiffer also recognizes the remarkable power of new technologies in expanding the reach and effectiveness of training. While e-hype has often created whizbang solutions in search of a problem, we are dedicated to bringing convenience and enhancements to proven training solutions. All our e-tools comply with rigorous functionality standards. The most appropriate technology wrapped around essential content yields the perfect solution for today's on-the-go trainers and human resource professionals.

Pfeiffer
www.pfeiffer.com   *Essential resources for training and HR professionals*

75
e-Learning
Activities

Making Online Learning Interactive

Ryan Watkins

Pfeiffer
A Wiley Imprint
www.pfeiffer.com

ISBN: 0–7879–7585–0

Library of Congress Cataloging-in-Publication Data
Watkins, Ryan.
75 e-learning activities: making online learning interactive / Ryan Watkins.
p. cm.
Includes bibliographical references and index.
ISBN 0–7879–7585–0 (alk. paper)
1. Education—Computer network resources. 2. Internet in education. 3. Interactive multimedia.
I. Title: Seventy-five e-learning activities. II. Title.
LB1044.87.W38 2005
371.33'467'8—dc22   2004022989

Acquiring Editor: Matthew Davis
Director of Development: Kathleen Dolan Davies
Developmental Editor: Susan Rachmeler
Editor: Rebecca Taff
Senior Production Editor: Dawn Kilgore
Manufacturing Supervisor: Becky Carreno

Printed in Mexico
Printing 10   9   8   7   6   5   4

Contents

Section One: Tips for Effective e-Learning Design and Delivery   19

Section Two: Introductions and Icebreakers   39

Section Three: e-Learning Skills   83

Section Four: Collaboration and Team Building   123

Section Five: Elaborating on Course Content 145

Section Six: Increasing Interactivity 213

Acknowledgments

I WOULD LIKE TO EXPRESS my appreciation and gratitude for the encouragement I have received from friends and family throughout the writing of this book. I would especially like to thank the following people for their support: Doug and Judi Watkins, Monte and Julie Watkins, and Christina Gee.

In addition, the contributions of Mel Silberman and Steve Sugar add great value to the book, and working with both of them was a great pleasure.

I am also grateful for the many colleagues and students who have participated in the development of the activities and tips that are found in this book, including the online students of the Educational Technology Leadership program at The George Washington University, Mike Corry, Diane Atkinson, Amy Lynch, Chih Tu, Bill Robie, Bruce Roemmelt, Ralph Mueller, Mary Futrell, and Stephen Joel Trachtenberg (The George Washington University); Doug Leigh (Pepperdine University); Roger Kaufman and Leon Sims (Florida State University); Mike Simonson, Charlie Schlosser, Marsha Burmeister, and Mary Ellen Maher (Nova Southeastern University); Lya, Jan, and Yusra Visser (Learning Development, Inc.); and Atsusi Hirumi (University of Central Florida).

Lastly, I would like to acknowledge all of those at Pfeiffer who have contributed to the success of the book, including Matt Davis, Kathleen Dolan Davies, Susan Rachmeler, Dawn Kilgore, and Laura Reizman.

Introduction

Getting the Most from This Resource

Creative ideas lead to engaging, entertaining, interactive, meaningful, and valuable course experiences. . . both in the traditional training classroom as well as in the high-tech online classroom.

Regrettably, however, creative ideas are not always easy for us to come by when we are designing, developing, or teaching an online course. While most of us can see the value of including engaging activities in our e-learning courses, the ideas (and the details) for how those can be integrated often escape us while we are under pressure to have the course available to learners "yesterday."

The activities included in this book offer online course developers, instructors, and trainers, for the first time, comparable resources for generating creative and interactive course experiences that trainers, teachers, professors, and others have had access to for years when it comes to traditional classroom courses. By identifying a variety of activities that can be used to create meaningful and engaging online course experiences, this book will "stir the creativity" of anyone who is looking to bring interactivity to their online courses.

What Are e-Learning Activities?

Online courses do not have to be the electronic adaptation of the traditional correspondence course in which interactivity and engagement have often been lacking. In contrast, online courses can effectively use Internet technologies to facilitate e-learning that is exciting, interactive, purposeful, and beneficial for online learners.

e-Learning activities use online technologies, such as chat rooms, discussion boards, or email, to facilitate participation of e-learners in meaningful exercises related to the course and its learning objectives. Much like the activities and games used in traditional classroom training, e-learning activities can be used by instructors and trainers to accomplish a variety of goals, such as introducing learners to one another, sharing experiences, benefiting from team learning, increasing participation, or encouraging learners to develop constructive online relationships throughout the course.

The e-learning activities presented in this book are a combination of both unique translations of traditional training activities (for example, Activity 1: Let Me Introduce. . .) as well as distinctive exercises that utilize online technologies that are not available in the traditional classroom (for example, Activity 9: Websites About Myself). By integrating these activities into your courses, you can transform your online courses into learning experiences where e-learners are immersed in thoughtful discussions, challenged by course content, motivated to work together as teams on interactive exercises, and involved in the development of the learning communities that are too often lost when courses are offered online. By adapting many of the familiar activities from the traditional classroom and utilizing many of the unique opportunities of online technology, this book provides numerous ideas for creating interactive online environments within most any e-learning course.

Each of the e-learning activities in this book is designed to create interactive online learning experiences. Consequently, these activities are not often applicable to self-paced individualized courses or courses that do not use at least one of the online communication technologies, such as email, chat rooms, or discussion boards. Although activities can be used to improve the engagement of learners in self-paced individualized courses, interactions with other learners are a necessary component for achieving many types of active learning (for example, full-class learning, stimulating discussions, team learning, peer teaching). For this reason, I have limited the focus of the e-learning activities in this book to those that generate purposeful interactions among e-learners and their online instructors.

What Can You Achieve with e-Learning Activities?

For most e-learners and online instructors alike, the e-learning classroom is a new environment that requires a variety of technology skills and communications strategies that are not the same as those used in previous classroom experiences. As a result, when working to overcome these challenges we often fail to remember that the online classroom can also be a creative, interactive, entertaining, and engaging environment. As a guide when you are designing and developing online courses, this book can unleash imaginative and resourceful ideas for hundreds of online activities that you can use to accomplish the learning objectives of most any online course.

By including a variety of interactive online experiences in your e-learning courses, you can improve retention rates, increase learner participation, achieve your learning objectives, develop online learning communities, and ensure that your online courses engage learners, regardless of the course topic.

Is This Book for Me?

- Are you currently or do you plan to *design* a course in which learners will have access to online technologies (for example, chat rooms, discussion boards, email)?

- Are you currently or do you plan to *develop* a course in which learners will have access to online technologies?

- Are you currently or do you plan to *teach* or *facilitate* a course in which learners will have access to online technologies?

- Are you currently or do you plan to facilitate or teach *classroom courses* in which learners will access online technologies before, during, or after the class?

- Are you currently or do you plan to facilitate or teach *entirely online courses* in which learners will access online technologies?

If you answered *yes* to any of these questions, then *this book is for you.*

Teachers, trainers, professors, instructional designers, and most any other professional involved in the design, development, or facilitation of courses that use online technologies can benefit from activities described in this book.

When Should I Use This Book?

In the competitive businesses of education and training, the design, development, and facilitation of courses is regularly done in nearly simultaneous cycles. As a result, today it is necessary for trainers, teachers, instructional designers, professors, and others to quickly identify and create activities and games that can be used to increase interactivity, engage learners, create online relationships, accomplish learning objectives, develop learning communities, and elaborate on course content through the use of online technologies. As a quick-reference guide, this book can be used at any point when you are designing, developing, or teaching an online course or a classroom course that uses online technologies to expand the learning experience.

How Can I Integrate e-Learning Activities into My Courses?

Having survived many education and training courses, most of us know that effective learning experiences are rarely those that rely solely on lectures of an instructor. As a result, similar principles that guide the development of active classroom training should be used to design effective online learning. Ideally, you will want to include a variety of e-learning activities (some small group activities and some large group activities, some real-time activities and some delayed response activities) throughout most any online course.

Of course, there are many considerations that must be made when designing an online learning experience that involves the active participation of learners, such as the learning objectives, the length of the course, the number of participants, the time committed to the course by individual learners, the familiarity of learners with online technologies, and your online communication and management skills as the instructor. Yet most online courses can benefit from the integration of one or more e-learning activities that meaningfully engage the learners in discussions related to the course content.

As with any instructional technique, e-learning activities are best included when they accomplish specified learning objectives. Hence, it is important to first define what learners will know and be able to do when they have completed the online training prior to selecting any of the activities, exercises, games, or other instructional techniques that will be used to accomplish those objectives. Only when the objectives have been defined, prioritized, and included in the instructional sequence is it time to consider the number, placement, and length of the e-learning activities that will be utilized to achieve the goals of the course. By designing your course experiences and activities entirely around the objectives to be achieved, you can better ensure that your learners benefit from the online learning experience.

When Should I Use e-Learning Activities?

If you are new to teaching online courses, my suggestion is that you first try using one of the Introduction and Icebreaker activities included in Section Two. These activities offer a variety of techniques for involving learners in discussions with their peers, and most are suitable for those new to the online technologies that are used in e-learning.

For both e-learners and online instructors, active participation in e-learning activities can require the use of study strategies, online communication skills, and technical skills that have not always been developed through experiences in the traditional classroom. As a result, even if there are struggles with completing the first activities that you integrate into the courses, don't be alarmed or apprehensive about including more activities in future lessons. As learners adapt to both the limitations and the opportunities of online learning and communications, their capacity to benefit from e-learning activities will mature, and the integration of additional activities will become a practical option as the active engagement of learners leads to the accomplishment of increasingly complex learning objectives.

Just as most of us would not want to sit through seven hours of lecture in a training workshop, neither do we want to read seven hours of transcribed lecture notes. That being said, however, most useful learning experiences are more than just a series of activities and games. As a result, online courses typically utilize e-learning activities to engage learners in active participation at times that are critical for accomplishing the course's learning objectives. Whether this is five activities during a course, or just one activity, is therefore dependent on the objectives to accomplished, the length of the course, the number of participants, the time commitment of learners, and other instructional design considerations.

Your first time teaching an online course will typically be the most difficult to include e-learning activities. Each subsequent time you teach the course, you can adjust the number, sequence, and length of the activities based on your previous experiences. As a result, my suggestion is to integrate at least two e-learning activities into each course the first time it is taught. This way you have ample opportunities to vary the number of activities or substitute alternative activities the next time the course is taught.

How Can I Be Sure That the e-Learning Activities Will Be Successful?

The success of any e-learning activity is dependent both on the active participation of the learners and the instructor. Accordingly, in order for an activity to be successful, first and foremost you must participate as the instructor. Although you may not always be actively posting to a discussion board or chat room, as the instructor you should be monitoring the participation and progress of learners throughout any e-learning activity.

Gaining the active participation of learners is accomplished both through the interest in the activity (that is, making it engaging and meaningful) and the integration of the activity with the other aspects of the course. As the saying goes, what gets measured gets done, and with e-learning activities it is often beneficial to associate some aspect of the learner's performance assessment with quality participation in the e-learning activities. My experience has been, however, that participation grades based on the number or length of postings alone most often are of little motivation to learners. Although the subjectivity of assessing quality participation is typically challenging, learners do appreciate efforts to assess the value of their performance when the instructor is actively and visibly involved throughout the course's activities.

Last, for online activities to be successful, both the instructor and the students must plan for the unexpected and remain flexible. Inevitably, online technologies will fail to function at some point during one of your e-learning activities. As an online instructor, you should have a contingency plan for what you, and the learners, should do when the technology fails to work as desired. Perhaps the plan is to use an alternative computer lab or to complete the activity using email instead of the chat room. In any case you should plan for the unavoidable technical problems that can occur. For example, when implementing an e-learning activity that uses an online chat room, I typically recommend that you let learners know that, if the chat room fails to work, then they should wait for an email from you letting them know how the activity will proceed until the chat room is working again. Not only does this reduce the potential stress on learners when technical glitches happen, but it also keeps your email inbox from filling up with questions about what to do next when the chat room fails to let participants post messages.

Just as you will want to be prepared for surprises as an online instructor, e-learners in your courses should also be prepared for unexpected technical glitches. Identifying alternative computer labs (for example, public libraries), having a notebook with contact information for technical support services, and saving back-up copies of important files can each save learners a great deal of frustration and time when technical issues arise.

e-Learning activities can add an exciting and meaningful dimension to an online course, and with a little contingency planning by both the instructor and learners, most technical problems can be overcome.

Where Should I Keep This Book?

Much as you keep your cookbooks near your kitchen, as a quick-reference guide this book is most useful when kept near you when you are designing, developing, or teaching online courses. For many of us, when creating or facilitating an online course, we struggle from time to time with course content that does not necessarily engage learners in the ways that we had hoped; that is a perfect time to use one or more of the activities from this book to restore the energy and interactivity that can make e-learning meaningful for online learners.

How Are the Activities Described?

Individual activities each contain ten discrete elements that will provide you with all of the necessary information for facilitating them in your online course:

1. *Activity Summary.* The activity summary provides you with a short description of the activity and how it can be used in an online course.

2. *Goals.* The goals detail what learners are expected to achieve during and after the activity.

3. *Collaborative Learning.* Collaborative learning identifies a recommended group size for the activity (individual, small group, large group).

4. *Recommended e-Learning Experience.* The recommended e-learning experience recognizes that, for both the instructor and the learner, some activities require additional familiarity with e-learning or technical skills in order to be successful. For novices, those instructors or learners who are new to e-learning and online technologies such as discussion boards and chat rooms, the activities will typically require fewer technical skills and less complex interactions. These activities are best suited for instructors or learners in their first or second online course. e-Learning activities that are recommended for experienced instructors or students, for example, moderate or advanced, are typically more demanding and work best when all participants are familiar with the online technologies being applied.

5. *Mode.* The mode for an activity is either synchronous (real time), asynchronous (delayed time), or both.

6. *Time Required.* The time required gives the estimated time necessary for learners to complete the activity.

7. *Materials.* The materials indicate which online technologies are required for the activity.

8. *Preparation.* Preparation describes those tasks that should be completed by the instructor prior to beginning the e-learning activity.

9. *Process.* Process details the steps that should be taken to facilitate the online activity.

10. *Facilitator Notes.* The facilitator notes offer a number of variations, tips, and suggestions for how e-learning activities can be developed and used in online courses.

How Should I Use the CD-ROM?

The CD-ROM included with this book has a number of files, in both rich text format (.rtf) and Adobe Acrobat format (.pdf), which can be used when facilitating e-learning activities. These include email templates, model instructions, and other resources that you may want to use as a starting place for your online activities.

Look for the CD-ROM icon in activities that have supplementary materials included on the enclosed CD.

How Is the Book Organized?

Much like a cookbook, the seventy-five e-learning activities included in this book are written as stand-alone recipes for both your success as an online instructor and the success of your students as e-learners. The selection matrix of the activities included at the end of this introduction can be used to determine which are most appropriate for accomplishing your learning objectives, depending on the number of learners in your course, the technology available to learners, and the amount of time you want learners to dedicate to energetic participation in the activity.

Before the individual activities are described, however, the book includes more than eighty practical tips and suggestions for increasing the interactivity in your online courses. From information on facilitating a synchronous chat to tips that you will want to share with learners in your course, this section of the book offers condensed guidelines for developing effective e-learning courses.

Following the tips are the seventy-five e-learning activities. These activities are organized into five sections based on how they can most effectively be used in a typical online course:

- Introductions and Icebreakers
- e-Learning Skills
- Collaboration and Team Building
- Elaborating on Course Content
- Increasing Interactivity

Although the activities are divided into five sections, I encourage you to mix and match them as you use them in your online courses. Often, you may want to use elements of one activity along with the rules of another activity to create a unique activity of your own.

The book also contains a glossary of essential e-learning terms along with non-technical definitions. Last, I have included a list of additional resources for instructors and trainers who want to create interactive training experiences.

How Can I Select an Appropriate e-Learning Activity?

The following selection matrix is a quick-reference guide to the activities that can be used to swiftly identify which activities are most likely to work best in your online course.

e-Learning Activities Selection Matrix

Introductions and Icebreakers

Activity Number	Group Size			Mode		Time Required			
	Small (1-7)	Medium (8-15)	Large (16+)	Asynchronous	Synchronous	1 day or less	2-3 days	3-5 days	6+ days
1	✓			✓			✓		
2			✓	✓			✓		
3			✓	✓			✓		
4			✓	✓				✓	
5		✓		✓				✓	
6			✓	✓				✓	
7			✓	✓			✓		
8			✓	✓	✓	✓			
9			✓	✓				✓	
10		✓		✓			✓		
11			✓	✓	✓		✓		
12			✓		✓	✓			
13			✓		✓	✓			

(continued)

Selection Matrix

Selection Matrix

e-Learning Activities Selection Matrix (continued)

Activity Number	Group Size			Mode		Time Required			
	Small (1-7)	Medium (8-15)	Large (16+)	Asynchronous	Synchronous	1 day or less	2-3 days	3-5 days	6+ days
e-Learning Skills									
14	✓			✓				✓	
15	✓			✓		✓			
16			✓	✓			✓		
17			✓	✓				✓	
18			✓	✓			✓	✓	
19		✓		✓			✓		
20	✓		✓	✓				✓	
21	✓			✓					
Collaboration and Team Building									
22	✓			✓			✓		
23		✓			✓	✓			
24			✓	✓				✓	
25			✓	✓			✓		
26		✓		✓				✓	

Selection Matrix

Activity Number	Group Size			Mode		Time Required			
	Small (1-7)	Medium (8-15)	Large (16+)	Asynchronous	Synchronous	1 day or less	2-3 days	3-5 days	6+ days
Elaborating on Course Content									
27	✓			✓		✓			
28	✓		✓		✓	✓			
29	✓	✓		✓			✓		
30	✓			✓			✓		
31		✓	✓		✓	✓		✓	
32	✓			✓			✓	✓	
33	✓			✓				✓	
34	✓			✓				✓	✓
35	✓			✓		✓			
36				✓					✓
37	✓			✓			✓		
38			✓	✓			✓	✓	
39			✓	✓			✓		
40		✓		✓					
41	✓			✓		✓			
42			✓	✓			✓	✓	
43			✓	✓					
44			✓	✓			✓		
45			✓	✓					✓
46				✓		✓			

(continued)

Selection Matrix

e-Learning Activities Selection Matrix (continued)

Activity Number	Group Size Small (1-7)	Group Size Medium (8-15)	Group Size Large (16+)	Mode Asynchronous	Mode Synchronous	Time Required 1 day or less	Time Required 2-3 days	Time Required 3-5 days	Time Required 6+ days
47	✓			✓				✓	✓
48	✓			✓	✓		✓		✓
49	✓			✓					
50			✓			✓			
51			✓		✓	✓			✓
52			✓		✓				
53			✓	✓	✓			✓	
54			✓	✓				✓	✓
55	✓			✓				✓	
56	✓			✓			✓		
57			✓	✓	✓	✓			
58	✓			✓				✓	
59	✓			✓				✓	
60		✓							✓

Increasing Interactivity

Selection Matrix

Activity Number	Group Size			Mode		Time Required			
	Small (1-7)	Medium (8-15)	Large (16+)	Asynchronous	Synchronous	1 day or less	2-3 days	3-5 days	6+ days
Increasing Interactivity *(continued)*									
61	✓		✓	✓			✓		
62	✓✓			✓				✓	✓
63	✓✓				✓	✓		✓	
64				✓				✓	
65	✓✓		✓	✓			✓	✓	
66	✓✓			✓					✓
67			✓	✓					✓
68					✓	✓			
69		✓			✓	✓			
70	✓✓		✓	✓		✓		✓	✓
71	✓✓		✓	✓		✓			✓
72	✓		✓	✓		✓			
73				✓				✓	
74				✓		✓	✓	✓	
75			✓		✓	✓			✓

Tips for Effective e-Learning Design and Delivery

....

BEFORE YOU ACTIVELY START TO DESIGN AND DELIVER AN INTERACTIVE E-LEARNING COURSE, you may first want to review this section. The tips included in this section offer a primer on creating interactive and meaningful online learning experiences; they are a condensed version of the many books on how to design and deliver e-learning. Most of the tips are well-known and not a revelation to instructors or trainers. Their application in online courses is, however, often unique and worth a review.

The majority of the tips included in the section are written for you and your perspective as the online instructor; yet many of the tips are also applicable to e-learners. Therefore, as you read through the tips, take time to consider each of them from the perspective of the online learner as well.

10 Tips for Assessing Learner Readiness

In order to design and deliver effective instruction, not only must you determine what is to be taught, but you must also resolve how the content can best be taught to the learners who will be completing the course. As a result, when developing online courses you want to consider many of the same prerequisite skills and learner characteristics that you would for a traditional classroom course (for example, previous courses, entry skills, attitudes toward content, motivation, ability levels, learning preferences), as well as the several proficiencies related to the unique demands of e-learning (for example, technical abilities, technology access, e-learning experience, online communication skills).

1. *Ask potential e-learners questions about their knowledge and skills related to specific technologies you plan to use in the online course.* For example: Do you know how to download plug-ins (for example, Flash®, Real Media® Player) for your Web browser? Have you saved bookmarks (or favorites) before?

2. *Ask potential e-learners questions about their specific experiences with e-learning.* For example: Have you taken an online course previously? What challenges did you encounter with previous e-learning experiences? What e-learning study skills have you developed?

3. *Ask potential e-learners questions about their specific experiences with topics related to the course content.* For example: Have you taken a formal course on the topic previously? Have you had the opportunity to apply similar materials in your work?

4. *Ask potential e-learners questions about their expectations for the course.* For example: What knowledge or skills do you hope to gain through this course? How do you plan to apply what you learn in the course in your work or other courses?

5. *Ask potential e-learners questions about the time they have available.* For example: How many hours per day/week do you have available for this course? What other commitments do you have that may keep you from participating online?

6. *Ask potential e-learners questions about their availability for synchronous (real time) activities.* For example: Would you be available on one or two weeknights during the course for synchronous *chats*?

7. *Ask potential e-learners questions about their Internet access.* For example: Do you have broad-band or dial-up Internet access? Do you have access to the Internet only at home? Can you identify one or two alternative sources for Internet access as a contingency if your home access is lost?

8. *Ask potential e-learners questions about online communications.* For example: Do you feel comfortable communicating with others using email? Have you previously participated in a synchronous chat room discussion?

9. *Ask potential e-learners questions about their software configuration.* For example: Do you currently use an Apple Macintosh® or Microsoft Windows® computer? Do you have access to Microsoft Word®? Adobe Acrobat®?

10. *Ask potential e-learners questions about their access to technical support.* For example, does your current Internet service provider offer technical support? Do you have a family member or friend who can help you if there are technical problems with your computer?

Bonus: The e-Learning Readiness Self-Assessment activity (in Section Three) can also be an effective technique for helping learners identify both their readiness for e-learning as well as the study habits and technical areas where they may want to further develop their skills.

10 Tips for Designing Effective e-Learning

The design and delivery of successful online courses is best accomplished through the application of a systematic instructional design process. From the analysis of course objectives and learners to the selection of an appropriate instructional strategy and the formative evaluation of course materials, an orderly process for developing course materials is essential for creating effective learning experiences. While sources for more information on instructional design are included in the Additional Resources section, the following tips can help you customize any course design process for the unique considerations of e-learning.

1. *Don't try to simulate the classroom.* Online courses are far more valuable when they are not created as the electronic adaptation of the traditional classroom course. Capitalizing on the unique opportunities offered by online technologies can make your course both distinctive and exceptional.

2. *Focus on results.* Effective online instruction is most often developed when the instructional designer, teacher, trainer, and/or facilitator maintain a focus on the results learners will achieve through the e-learning experience (that is, what learners will know and be able to do when the course is done).

3. *Link assessments to your objectives.* When you have defined what learners will know and be able to do after your online course is complete, these standards should then be used as criteria when you establish assessments of learner performance.

4. *Intersperse activities.* Like engaging classroom instruction, which is typically peppered with activities, interactive online courses use a variety of online activities to maintain learner enthusiasm throughout the course.

5. *Provide clear instructions and guidelines.* Descriptions of assign-ments, activities, projects, and other events in online courses should include straightforward instructions and guidelines for how the learner should complete the tasks.

6. *Keep the performance environment (the workplace) in mind.* Online courses are most successful when learners complete the experience with knowledge and skills that are applicable outside of the online classroom. Consequently, you should keep their post-course performance in mind while designing the activities, assignments, and course content.

7. *Compensate for missing nonverbal cues.* Online communications are rich with examples of miscommunications due to the missing nonverbal cues that many of us rely on in daily inter-actions. Yet most e-learners can overcome these challenges by planning what they want to communicate, asking a peer to proofread their communications, double-checking their mes-sages, using a dictionary, including emoticons, and applying a variety of other online strategies for effective communica-tions.

8. *Break the ice.* Online courses can fashion an environment in which learners build online relationships with their peers and enjoy a comfortable learning experience by encouraging learners to break the ice and interact with each other starting the first time they sign into the course.

9. *Create a template.* The efficient development of online materi-als can be facilitated by the creation of a template for each module, lesson, unit, or other element of a course. Your tem-plate could include such elements as news and notes, discus-sion questions, online resources, lesson activity, next steps, lecture, required readings, or links to review that will appear in every course module, lesson, or unit.

10. *Make time for feedback.* Successful online courses provide learners with a good amount of feedback on activities, assignments, and questions they have throughout the course. As a result you must plan your time wisely to facilitate these critical discussions.

10 Tips for Teaching Online

Online courses can be engaging, meaningful, and exciting experiences for learners and instructors alike. When online courses are interactive, e-learners and instructors can create valuable learning communities, build friendships, and share in online experiences that have similar characteristics and results as those of the traditional training classroom. The following ten tips will help bring active learning to your online courses.

1. *Establish clear expectations for participation.* The expectations for participation in a classroom course are typically recognizable through the course agenda, syllabus, or timeline. For online courses, however, these norms for participation are less frequently established or recognized by participants and should therefore be clarified.

2. *Provide etiquette guidelines for online communications.* Rules, policies, and recommendations for how participants should interact during an active online course are best communicated at the beginning of the course. For example, online communications should avoid sarcasm, idioms, jargon, and slang.

3. *Test-drive any and all technology.* Prior to assigning activities that use online technology (for example, chat room, discussion forum, streaming video), the associated tools should be tested by both you and the course participants. Identifying technical problems before course activities begin can save you time as well as a variety of hassles.

4. *Create an effective teaching environment.* Just as a loud radio or television would divert your attention while facilitating a classroom activity, online technologies (for example, email or instant messenger) can distract you from online engagement just as easily. Thus, it is best to avoid multitasking while teaching online.

5. *Don't try to do it all the first time.* Activities for creating engaging online courses are as numerous as your imagination, although too much of a good thing can often lead to problems for participants (for example, technology overload, confusion, technical problems).

6. *Write comments and questions in advance.* When teaching an online course, you should prepare for discussions, especially "live" chat room discussion, ahead of time using your word processing program. By typing questions or comments beforehand, you can simply cut and paste them into the chat room discussion at the appropriate time without having to delay the conversation.

7. *Require informative subject lines.* Given the volume of online communications in most e-learning courses, using and requiring detailed subject lines is essential to course organization and management.

8. *Involve participants.* The most frequent complaint of online learners is a feeling of isolation from the learning community. Involving learners through online groups, engaging activities, frequent discussion topics, and other active learning strategies can reduce the anxiety of participants by helping them establish online relationships with their peers.

9. *Review and reflect.* Online courses provide you and the participants with unprecedented documentation of what was taught, referenced, discussed, and decided in an online course, all of which can be used effectively to review and reflect on the course experiences.

10. *Expect the unexpected.* Any course that relies on technology will experience a variety of technical "melt-downs" from time to time (for example, power outages, Internet disconnections, chat room failures, software compatibility problems). Although technology contingency plans are vital, an online instructor must remain flexible and patient. For example, if an e-learner is not able to attend a one-time synchronous chat due to a power outage, you may want to have a comparable assignment available to ensure that the learner can achieve the related course objectives.

10 Tips for Using Email*

Email is almost certainly the most common online communication tool used in e-learning courses. Despite the fact that you—and your course participants—likely have a great deal of experience in communicating with friends and family using email, the use of email in online courses should not be overlooked in preparing for success.

1. *Check—and double-check—recipient lists.* Always review the To:, Cc:, and Bcc: fields prior to sending any email. Often, in a hurry to complete our work, we may mistakenly add or omit an intended recipient to an email message. This can be both embarrassing (such as when an email to another instructor goes to a learner) and sometimes destructive to the online relationships you have built with course participants.

2. *Include previous message in replies.* Often you will want to quote the original message in your reply email in order to avoid possible miscommunications. When including an original message in the reply, however, do not alter the original message in any way. In addition, typically you will want to include only the prior message (that is, do not include the previous five messages in your reply).

3. *Don't reply immediately, at least at first.* Although we will often-times want to respond to learner questions immediately, doing this at the beginning of a course may set the expectation among course participants that you will respond instantly to emails throughout the course, which will become more challenging as more activities and assignments are submitted for feedback. As an online instructor you should establish and communicate desired norms, holding your learners to the same standards that you set for yourself (for example, a maximum of 48 or 72 hours to respond).

*Based on Watkins and Corry (2005).

4. *Describe attachments.* In your email messages that include an attached file, a description of the attached files (including the name of the file and the software application used to create the file) should always be included.

5. *Only forward course-relevant emails.* Avoid forwarding email messages that do not directly relate to the course materials; jokes and other miscellaneous emails should be saved for personal emails only.

6. *Don't store all your emails in the inbox.* Your email inbox will quickly become full of old messages and you will have a difficult time accessing important information if you do not develop a folder structure for storing email messages. When a message comes to your email inbox, reply to it and save it in an appropriate folder that day.

7. *Resist over-analysis.* Try not to read too much into the statements of learners or take comments too personally. Miscommunications are common in online communications since many of the everyday nonverbal communication cues (such as eye contact or body gestures) are not available.

8. *Have multiple email accounts.* You should have a separate email account for each online course that you facilitate, as well as an independent email account for personal email.

9. *Number tasks, lists, and questions.* Many of us have developed the poor habit of primarily scanning email messages and not reading each message carefully. To more effectively communicate with online learners, number or bullet tasks to be completed or questions to be answered.

10. *Use formatting to emphasize your ideas.* Use the bold, underline, and italics features of your email software applications to communicate more effectively with learners. For example, if you want learners to note the date and time that an assignment is due, make the information bold in your email.

10 Tips for Using Synchronous Chats*

Real-time (or synchronous) chats provide online courses with one of the few experiences where participants can receive immediate replies to questions or comments, thus allowing for a conversation to develop quickly and important issues to be discussed. For that reason you will want to use this unique technology in a manner that takes advantage of those opportunities.

1. *Provide etiquette guidelines and chat rules.* Guidelines and rules for how the *chat* will be facilitated are a required component of most successful chat room discussions. Your etiquette guide should include such topics as the order of questions, how to address questions or comments, raising your hand or gaining attention, private discussions, as well as an agenda for the discussion. You can even use the tips below as a basis for your guidelines.

2. *Don't greet or say goodbye to everyone.* Most synchronous chat software provides a list of who has entered or left the *chat* room, so do not greet each new person with a "hello" when he or she arrives or feel that it is necessary to post a "goodbye" message when you are leaving the chat.

3. *Don't respond to every message.* Respond only to those that address you specifically or to which your response will make a value contribution to the discussion; even as the instructor you do not have to respond to all participant postings.

4. *Address questions or comments to the intended recipient.* Identify the individual you would like to respond or ask a question of when posting to the chat discussion.

*Based on Watkins and Corry (2005).

5. *Write comments and questions in advance.* When teaching an online course, you should prepare for discussions, especially "live" chat room discussion, ahead of time using your word processing program. By typing questions or comments beforehand, you can simply cut and paste them into the chat room discussion at the appropriate time without having to delay the conversation.

6. *Keep postings concise.* To the extent possible, keep questions or comments short and to the point. If a question or comment is likely to take up more lines of text than are visible in the chat interface, then divide the question into two parts.

7. *Don't try to multi-task.* Just as a loud radio or television would divert your attention while facilitating a classroom activity, online technologies (email, instant messenger, Web surfing) can distract you from online engagement just as easily. Thus it is best to avoid multi-tasking while participating in online chat.

8. *Leave irrelevant spelling or grammar errors.* If you do misspell a word when posting to a chat, do not post another message correcting the misspelling—unless the misspelled word would significantly change the meaning of the message.

9. *Avoid sarcasm, idioms, slang, and jokes.* Do not use cultural or regional communication techniques that can easily result in miscommunication.

10. *Keep a record or transcript.* Often the transcripts or records of what was discussed and decided during a synchronous chat will be of value later in the online course; keeping a record of the conversation can be critical.

10 Tips for Using Asynchronous Discussion Boards*

Participants in an asynchronous discussion board conversation can choose when they reply to the latest additions to the discussion; as a result, the pace and length of the conversation can vary greatly. With some planning, however, the delayed pace of the discussion board can be used to create an engaging and rich conversation with learners on most course topics.

1. *Clarify expectations for participation.* Clear guidelines for how often learners should participate in a discussion board conversation should be communicated (for example, once a day, twice a day, twice a week), along with information on how the quality of their participation will be assessed.

2. *Create a schedule for participation.* Schedule times throughout each discussion board activity when you will participate in the conversation. Include in this plan how much time you will spend responding to postings with your comments or questions.

3. *Don't respond to everyone and all postings.* Even as the facilitator of an online course, you will want to respond only to those postings that address you specifically or to which your response will make a valuable contribution to the discussion. Find a balance of quality and quantity with your additions to the discussion.

4. *Use the subject line (and require learners to do so as well).* In order to reduce the amount of time and effort required for reviewing discussion board postings, it is important to include with each of your postings a summary description of the posting in the subject line.

*Based on Watkins and Corry (2005).

5. *Check spelling and grammar.* Since spelling and grammar are important in most communications, and since asynchronous communication allows the time, you should carefully check for errors and may want to use a word processing program to draft your postings before copying and pasting them into the discussion.

6. *Resist over-analysis.* Try not to read too much into the statements of learners or take comments too personally. Miscommunications are common in online communications since many of the everyday nonverbal communication cues (such as eye contact or body gestures) are not available.

7. *Provide a signature line (with email for private responses).* Although most discussion boards will include your name with each response you post, it is always a good idea to include your name and email at the end of your messages so learners can contact you privately if they have questions or want additional information that may not be pertinent to the course's discussion.

8. *Take your time.* Editing and reviewing your additions to the discussion board can help you to avoid miscommunications. Having time to revise and improve your comments or questions is a benefit of asynchronous discussions that you will want to use to your advantage (for example, adding links to Web resources or connecting current discussions with content from previous lessons).

9. *Lead by example.* Ensure that each of your postings to the discussion board is of the quality and length that you expect from learners; typically they will copy the communication style that you choose for your postings.

10. *Keep a record.* If discussion board postings will not remain available throughout the course and you would like to keep information contained in one or more of the postings, be sure to copy the posting(s) to a word processing document that you can save to your personal computer.

10 Tips for Your e-Learners*

Whether we realize it or not, over the years each of us has developed a set of learning skills and study habits we use to succeed in conventional classroom training. Many of these skills will, however, have to be transformed in order for us to have the same levels of success in online courses. The following tips, which can be distributed to your participants, can assist them in developing useful and practical skills for becoming effective e-learners.

1. *Establish reasonable goals and expectations.* The online classroom requires many unique study skills and learning strategies; consequently, you will want to establish goals and expectations that are reasonable based on your experiences both as a traditional classroom learner and as an e-learner. For example, do not panic if at first you struggle with the pace of the online discussions since learning the skills to adeptly communicate online takes practice.

2. *Learn the basics.* In order to be an effective online learner, you do not have to get a degree in the computer sciences, although developing a basic level of knowledge regarding how a computer and the Internet function can be useful throughout most any online course. Taking the time to learn the key terms and basic functions of the Internet can help you communicate effectively with your instructor, peers, and even technical support staff if you should require their assistance.

*Based on Watkins and Corry (2005).

3. *Have patience.* Neither your online instructor nor peers will be available online 24 hours a day, so you must be patient when waiting for responses to emails or discussion board postings. Most online courses will have guidelines or will work to establish group norms regarding the maximum response time that should be expected for class participation (for example, 48 or 72 hours). You should work to adhere to these standards.

4. *Be friendly and get to know peers.* The social life of an online learner can be active, stimulating, entertaining, and fun, but it doesn't happen without some directed effort. For example, email other participants in the course to ask questions, share ideas, or organize study groups.

5. *Schedule your study times.* Schedule times throughout the course when you will participate in the online conversations, complete assignments, participate in activities, and read required materials. Whether it is Monday, Wednesday, and Saturday afternoons or Tuesday, Thursday, and Sunday mornings, having scheduled time for course participation will keep you on track to success.

6. *Create a positive online study environment.* Like the physical study environment, the online study environment you create for completing your coursework will be critical to your success. In planning for success you will want to create an ideal online study environment that can aid in reducing distractions and increasing your comprehension of essential course information. For example, when reading online course materials turn off your instant messenger and email programs since these can be a distraction.

7. *Don't panic when technology fails.* The odds are very high that at some point during your online course a technical tool used for the course will not work as it should. Don't panic; simply take detailed notes of any error messages that you receive and contact the appropriate technical services group (for example, for Internet connectivity problems you would contact your Internet provider; for software failures you should contact the software manufacturer). After you have contacted the appropriate technical service group, you should then inform your instructor of the problem.

8. *Manage your time.* Procrastination, taking on the responsibilities of others, waiting for perfection, misusing free time, and other traditional challenges to effective time management also plague online learners. Yet through skillful planning and using technology to your advantage, you can overcome many of these obstacles to success. For example, you can use shared online calendars (for example, calendar.yahoo.com, www.calendars.net) to organize and plan study group discussions.

9. *Test-drive any and all technology.* Prior to completing any activity or assignment that uses online technology (chat room, discussion forum, streaming video), you should test the associated tools to ensure that they will work when it is time to participate in the course. Identifying technical problems before course activities begin can save you time as well as a variety of hassles.

10. *Participate and stay involved.* As an online learner it is your responsibility to remain involved in course discussion and activities, just as it your responsibility to attend sessions of classroom courses. Your active participation in the course will not only increase how much you learn from the course, but also boost your enjoyment of the online experience.

Section Two
Introductions
and Icebreakers

··

THE FIRST FEW HOURS AND DAYS of any course are often the most challenging for instructors and learners alike. During this period, early in the course, as the instructor you will want to establish constructive norms, initiate a positive tone to communications, demonstrate active participation, and help learners build beneficial relationships with their peers as they form a learning community. Since both good and bad habits are typically hard to break, establishing productive standards and norms during this period early in the course is essential.

To help you meet these challenges that occur at the beginning of any course, the Introductions and Icebreakers section includes a variety of e-learning activities that can be used to establish norms and build relationships among the learners in your online courses. The activities in this section can be used with learners with minimal e-learning experience (that is, novices) and offer a range of techniques for engaging learners in online conversations with their peers.

1

Let Me Introduce. . .

Activity Summary

The process of interviewing one's peers in an online course can be an effective tool for building online relationships and offer an alternative to the more commonly used posting of a personal biographical sketch. The Let Me Introduce. . . activity provides a structured process for learners to interview their peers and share the results with others in the course.

Goals

- Learners will conduct interviews in an effort to meet other learners in the course
- Learners will develop effective online communication skills for conducting interviews
- Learners will build communication skills for interacting with other learners throughout the remainder of the course

Collaborative Learning

Pairs of learners

Recommended e-Learning Experience

Learner—Novice
Facilitator—Novice

Mode

Asynchronous

Time Required

Two to three days (once-a-day minimum learner participation)

Materials

- Facilitator and learner access to an online asynchronous discussion board
- Facilitator and learner access to email
- (Optional) Learner access to a synchronous chat room

Preparation

1. Identify pairs of learners to work collaboratively during the activity.
2. Create two forums in the course's asynchronous discussion board: one for interviews and one for introductions.

Process

1. Require each learner to prepare at least five questions to be asked during the interview of his or her partner. The interview questions should provide the necessary information for making an interesting and informative introduction of the partner to the other learners in the course. For example, interview questions could include:
   - What experience do you have as an e-learner?
   - Have your previous e-learning experiences been positive or negative?
   - What expectations do you have for the course?
   - How do you plan to apply what we learn in this course?
   - What is your favorite website?
   - What about you would peers in the course find interesting?

2. Email learners in the course with directions for the activity and the names of their partners for the activity.

3. Have each learner interview his or her partner for the activity using email, an asynchronous discussion board, or a synchronous chat room discussion.

4. Have learners create and present two- to three-paragraph introductions of their partners to the other learners in the course.

5. Have learners post their introductions to the second forum you created in the discussion board.

6. Require that the subject line for each introduction include "Let me introduce. . . [the partner's name]."

7. After posting the introductions they created based on the interviews of their partners, have learners review the introductions of other learners in the course. When learners have questions or share common interests, then additional postings (replies) can be added to the forum in the discussion board.

Facilitator Notes

- If there are an odd number of learners in your course, assign a learner to be your partner for the activity. Hence, he or she will interview and introduce you for the activity and you will interview and introduce him or her.

- As a variation, use the round-robin approach with groups of three or four learners: learner A interviews and introduces learner B, learner B then interviews and introduces learner C, and learner C interviews and introduces learner A.

2

My First Time*

Activity Summary

Through the sharing of experiences as e-learners and users of online technology, the My First Time activity facilitates the introduction of learners and the development of an online learning community. In addition, the learner descriptions of their past experiences offer the facilitator a unique opportunity to assess the technology skills and online study habits of learners in the class.

Goals

- Learners will interact online in order to meet other learners in the course
- Learners will share their previous experiences as e-learners and users of technology
- Learners will build skills for interacting with other learners in the course

Collaborative Learning

Large groups (all learners in a course)

Recommended e-Learning Experience

Learner—Novice
Facilitator—Novice

*Developed in collaboration with Steve Sugar.

Mode

Asynchronous

Time Required

Two to three days (once-a-day minimum learner participation)

Materials

Facilitator and learner access to an online asynchronous discussion board

Preparation

1. Identify five to seven first-time experiences that learners in the course may have had as e-learners or users of technology. Possible first-time events could include:

   - My first time in an online course. . .
   - My first time in a synchronous chat room. . .
   - My first time using an asynchronous discussion board. . .
   - My first time buying something online. . .
   - My first time sending an email. . .
   - My first time using an Internet search engine. . .
   - My first time making travel reservations online. . .
   - My first time using a computer. . .
   - My first time downloading shareware. . .
   - My first time surfing the World Wide Web. . .

2. Create a forum in the course's asynchronous discussion board for each My First Time event you have identified for the activity.

Process

1. Require learners to respond to at least three of the My First Time experiences.

2. Have learners include in their responses a short description of what they remember about using the specified technology for the first time. For example:

   "My first time surfing the World Wide Web. . . was in 1993. My roommate had been given a computer for the holidays and had just installed a modem. We located a webpage and started to wait for the images to appear on screen. Two hours later we viewed a small black and white picture of the Moscow skyline and were amazed by how useful the computer had become."

3. Post two or three of your First Time experiences to the discussion forums as well.

4. Encourage participants to review and comment on the experiences of their peers.

Facilitator Notes

The My First Time activity doesn't have to be limited to online experiences. If you prefer, you may use other course-related topics to encourage learner participation. For example, in a leadership course you may want to include experiences like, "My first time managing a group of employees. . .," "My first time challenging my boss's decision. . .," or "My first time leading a meeting. . . ."

3

Likes and Dislikes

Activity Summary

As an icebreaker, the Likes and Dislikes activity can be used to familiarize learners with their peers and at the same time open the discussion of group norms and etiquette within the course. The activity builds on the previous experiences of learners in order to identify expectations and address concerns.

Goals

- Learners will examine their expectations and desires for the online course
- Learners will identify the necessary norms for the online course
- Learners will negotiate preliminary group norms for the course
- Learners will gain skills in effectively communicating using an online asynchronous discussion board

Collaborative Learning

Large groups (all learners in a course, or groups of 20 to 25)

Recommended e-Learning Experience

Learner—Novice
Facilitator—Novice

Mode
Asynchronous

Time Required
Two to three days (once-a-day minimum learner participation)

Materials
Facilitator and learner access to an online asynchronous discussion board

Preparation
Create a forum in the course's online asynchronous discussion board.

Process
1. Assign learners the task of posting to the discussion forum in the next 24 hours:
   - At least three attributes of online learning that they Like (for example, the flexibility to participate after work), and
   - At least three attributes of online learning that they Dislike (for example, technical problems can disrupt learning)
2. Request that learners do not discuss the Likes and Dislikes at this time, but just list them in their responses.
3. When at least 25 percent of the learners in the course identify or concur with a specific Like or Dislike, create a new discussion forum for additional discussion of that specific Like or Dislike.

4. Have learners discuss in each new forum both (a) how the attributes of online courses that learners Like can be included in the group's norms during the course, and (b) how attributes of online courses that learners Dislike can be avoided or addressed through the group's norms during the course.

5. Each time a Like or Dislike from the initial discussion forum is identified by at least a quarter of the learners in the course, another forum for discussing how to address that attribute of online learning should be established. By the end of the activity you should have four or five additional discussion forums for Likes and Dislikes.

Facilitator Notes

You may also use online survey or polling tools to shorten the activity by having learners quickly contribute to the discussion by ranking their Likes and Dislikes.

4

....

Worth a Thousand Words

Activity Summary

The Worth a Thousand Words activity utilizes the wise saying that "a picture is worth a thousand words" to give online learners the opportunity to use pictures, images, and illustrations from the World Wide Web to introduce themselves to other learners in the course.

Goals

- Learners will use images and pictures to illustrate their interests, background, and/or experiences
- Learners will communicate online using more than just text
- Learners will build skills for interacting online with their peers

Collaborative Learning

Large groups (all learners in a course)

Recommended e-Learning Experience

Learner—Novice
Facilitator—Novice

Mode

Asynchronous

Time Required

Three to five days (once-a-day minimum learner participation)

Materials

- Facilitator and learner access to an online asynchronous discussion board
- Learner access to the World Wide Web
- Facilitator and learner access to email.

Preparation

1. Create a forum in the course's online asynchronous discussion board.

2. Prepare instructions for learners on how to copy a picture from the World Wide Web and post them in the course's asynchronous discussion board. For example:

   "In order to copy a picture from the Web when you are using Microsoft Internet Explorer, you start by placing your cursor (that is, mouse) over the image that you want to copy. By then pressing the right-hand mouse button, you will be able to select from a menu of functions. Selecting the 'Save Picture As' option from the menu will allow you to save the picture's file to your computer's hard disk drive.

   "From this point, each course's asynchronous discussion board will require unique instructions on attaching (that is, uploading) the saved files to a posting in the discussion board. If you are not familiar with the process for attaching files to postings when using your course's discussion board software (for example, Blackboard®, WebCT®, Learning-Space®, First Class®) you should review the software manual or contact technical support services."

Process

1. Post to the discussion forum three images or pictures that illustrate your interests, background, and/or experiences as a model for learners, including a short discussion about why you chose the images.

2. Have learners identify three to five pictures or images from the World Wide Web that they believe illustrate their interests, background, and/or experiences.

3. Have learners copy the pictures or images to their computers.

4. Require learners to post to the discussion forum messages that have their images or pictures attached, and that include a short discussion of why they selected those specific images and pictures.

5. Encourage learners to review the Worth a Thousand Words activities of their peers and use these as a tool for getting to know one another.

Facilitator Notes

The Worth a Thousand Words activity could also be used in activities that are not icebreakers. You can even encourage learners to attach images and illustrations to their discussion postings throughout the course.

5

Find Someone Who. . .

Activity Summary

To engage learners and build community in any online course, you can use this online variation of the familiar training or classroom activity for motivating learners to actively seek out and meet other learners in the course.

Goals

- Learners will ask questions and provide answers to other learners in an effort to meet other learners in the course
- Learners will identify at least one interesting fact about each of several peers in the course
- Learners will be comfortable interacting with other learners throughout the remainder of the course

Collaborative Learning

Medium groups (8 to 15 learners)

Recommended e-Learning Experience

Learner—Novice
Facilitator—Novice

Mode

Asynchronous

Time Required

Three to five days (once-a-day minimum learner participation)

Materials

- Facilitator and learner access to an online asynchronous discussion board
- Facilitator and learner access to email

Preparation

1. Request that each learner in the course identify and email you a characteristic, experience, and/or possession that other learners in the course are unlikely to know about them. For example, a bachelor's degree in business, a red sports car, three children, more than three computers at home, administers his or her own webpage.

2. Randomly assign the characteristics, experiences, and/or possessions to learners in the course, ensuring that learners are not assigned their own.

3. Create a forum in the course's asynchronous discussion board for the activity.

Process

1. Email learners the characteristic, experience, or possession whose owner they are to locate among the learners in the course.

2. Instruct learners that they cannot reveal to other learners the characteristic, experience, or possession they are searching for in the activity. That is to say, learners cannot post a question to the discussion board asking for the names of learners who have, for example, children in college or a red sports car. They can only ask related questions that would provide them with clues about those individuals who meet the requirements of their search. For example, a learner may ask on the discussion board which learners have children who recently moved away from home or have an interest in sports cars.

3. Monitor the discussion forum to ensure that learners are not asking questions that give away the characteristic, experience, or possession they are searching for in the activity.

4. Once learners believe that they know which other learner has their assigned characteristic, experience, or possession, they should post the names in the discussion forum.

5. Have learners review the posting to determine whether they were accurately selected as having the characteristic, experience, or possession they had submitted.

Facilitator Notes

As a variation on the activity, have learners search for a variety of course-related information among their fellow learners using similar interactive activities. For example, learners can search for previous training experiences among their fellow learners in order to improve the sharing of information related to skills learners possess.

6

Tour My Favorite Website

Activity Summary

The Tour My Favorite Website activity is an asynchronous variation of the more familiar synchronous virtual tours that are guided by the facilitator. By having learners create the tours, this activity can be used as an icebreaker or as a tool for learners to share online resources related to course content with their peers.

Goals

- Learners will identify interesting and/or useful online resources
- Learners will present asynchronous tours to their fellow learners of websites they have identified
- Learners will gain skills for discovering useful information when visiting websites

Collaborative Learning

Large groups (all learners in a course)

Recommended e-Learning Experience

Learner—Novice
Facilitator—Moderate

Mode

Asynchronous

Time Required

Three to five days

Materials

- Facilitator and learner access to an online asynchronous discussion board
- Facilitator and learner access to email

Preparation

1. Create a forum in the course's asynchronous discussion board.

2. Develop a sample asynchronous virtual tour of your favorite website or the course website to illustrate the requirements of the activity for learners.

   The following is short example of a partial asynchronous virtual tour:

   "The Weather Channel's website, <http://www.weather.com>, is my favorite website. You could say that I am somewhat of a weather fanatic. Before the website was available my family and I typically left the television on the Weather Channel most of the day.

   "When you go to the main page of weather.com, you will find the national weather map and links to resources related to seasonal environmental conditions (for example, ski reports, foliage updates, and winter weather warnings).

"You can also use your local zip code (or the zip code of a location you may be visiting) to get the latest weather report. When you enter the zip code of interest in the box (top left of webpage), you will then receive a more detailed weather report for that location.

"Since the weather reports are continually being updated, I cannot provide a static link that will always show a report of your local weather. But do try entering your zip code.

"In addition, you can also get hourly weather predictions for your local area. You can access this information using the 'Hourly' button at the top of the 10-Day Forecast.

"As I mentioned previously, you can also get seasonal weather information with travel advisories, health reports, and gardening tips. These links are at the top of the main website. For a listing of these available features you can visit the 'Activities' webpage.

"See <http://www.weather.com/activities/>

"I hope that you enjoyed this abridged tour of my favorite website."

Process

1. Have each learner identify one website that he or she would consider to be one of his or her favorites (that is, one that characterizes his or her interests or profession, or one that is fun to visit).

2. Have learners develop an asynchronous tour of the website that describes what they like best about the site as well as highlights any useful functions that the website may offer.

3. Have learners post their tour to the asynchronous discussion board.

4. Encourage learners to participate in the asynchronous virtual tours created by their peers in the course.

Facilitator Notes

- The Tour My Favorite Website activity can also be done as a course content-related activity. As a content-related activity, learners should identify websites that are related to course topics. These could include searchable databases, information sites, online tools, and other Internet resources that learners find useful.

- The activity could also be done using synchronous tours, where learners use a synchronous chat room to guide their peers through the tour of their favorite website in real time.

7

Common Interests

Activity Summary

The Common Interests activity offers learners in an online course the opportunity to identify shared interests and common characteristics they have with their peers in the group. This activity can be used to encourage learners to participate in online discussions with their peers and form online relationships within most any size group.

Goals

- Learners will ask questions and provide answers to other students in an effort to meet other learners in the course
- Learners will identify at least one shared interest with several other learners in the course
- Learners will be comfortable interacting with their peers throughout the remainder of the course

Collaborative Learning

Large groups (all learners in a course)

Recommended e-Learning Experience

Learner—Novice
Facilitator—Novice

Mode

Asynchronous

Time Required

Two to three days (once-a-day minimum learner participation)

Materials

Facilitator and learner access to an online asynchronous discussion board

Preparation

1. Identify at least six to eight topics that learners can use to begin their exploration of what they have in common with the fellow learners in the course. Below is a list of possible topic areas:

   - My favorite website is. . .
   - I like to collect. . .
   - My favorite place to vacation is. . .
   - The food I like best is. . .
   - My favorite course was. . .
   - The thing I liked most about my last course was. . .
   - My hobby is. . .
   - My favorite sport to watch is. . .
   - My favorite sport to play is. . .
   - My pet likes to. . .
   - The best part of my job is. . .
   - On weekends I like to. . .
   - A great book is. . .
   - My favorite movie is. . .
   - I am from. . .

2. Create at least six to eight forums in the course's online asynchronous discussion board.

3. Post one of the discussion topics as the subject for each discussion forum.

4. Include a final forum that is open for learners to post comments that relate to their interest that may not have been included in your list.

Process

1. Have learners reply to at least four or five of the topic areas that you have posted within the discussion board. The postings of learners should include a short description of their related interests. For example, a response could be "My hobby is . . . cooking. Each year I try to learn how to cook foods from a new ethnic region of the world. This year I am trying to cook Lebanese foods."

2. Require learners to include a short description of their interest as the subject line to their posting. For example, "My pet likes to watch birds" or "I collect antique toys."

3. Participate in the discussion by posting your own interests.

Facilitator Notes

You can also use the discussion board for learners to identify similarities they may have with regard to course-related topics. For example, you could include in the topic areas for discussion "The most useful part of Chapter 2 was. . .," "In my job I can most easily apply. . .," or "I found the discussion of . . . to be most challenging in the course readings."

8

Composite Biography*

Activity Summary

As a tool for encouraging learners to participate in a course's synchronous chat rooms, you can use the Composite Biography activity to have learners share information, build an online community around their shared experiences, and explore the diversity among the learners in the course.

Goals

- Learners will contribute to a composite biography
- Learners will examine the diversity of experiences and backgrounds among other learners in the course
- Learners will build skills for interacting online with other learners

Collaborative Learning

Large groups (all learners in a course)

Recommended e-Learning Experience

Learner—Novice
Facilitator—Novice

Mode

Synchronous and Asynchronous

*Developed in collaboration with Steve Sugar.

Time Required

One day

Materials

- Facilitator and learner access to an online asynchronous discussion board
- Facilitator and learner access to an online synchronous chat room

Preparation

1. Identify a synchronous chat room for the activity. Most online course delivery tools (for example, Blackboard®, WebCT®, LearningSpace®) offer multiple chat rooms that can be used simultaneously for group activities or alone for whole-class activities. From the available chat rooms you should select a specific chat room (that is, chat room one or chat room A) for the activity.
2. Create a forum in the course's asynchronous discussion board.
3. Determine a date and time when the greatest number of learners in the course can participate in a synchronous conversation.
4. Create a list of learners in the course (for example, alphabetical, reversed-alphabetical, by registration date).

Process

1. Email learners with instructions for attending the synchronous chat discussion and participating in the activity. Include in the email the ordered list of learners in the course, since this will be the order in which learners are to participate in the synchronous discussion.

2. Enter the synchronous chat room at least 5 minutes prior to beginning the activity.

3. Begin the activity by posting a one-sentence description of a personal characteristic (for example, "I am the younger of two boys in my family"; "I attended a public high school in Massachusetts"; "I spent three years working on a ranch in Arizona").

4. Ask each learner to post, one at a time in order, a one-sentence description of one personal characteristic he or she would like to add to the composite biography. Each learner's one-sentence description should be unique, and not contradict any earlier postings (that is, when one learner has posted a description of where he went to college, no other learners can post a description that contradicts this by saying she went to another college). In the end, there should be the same number of single-sentence descriptions of personal characteristics as there are learners in the course.

5. Copy the entire set of postings from the chat room.

6. Paste a copy of the composite biography you have copied from the chat room into the asynchronous discussion forum.

7. Have learners review the composite biography and post to the discussion forum a one-paragraph description of the diversity within the course.

Facilitator Notes

If you cannot identify a convenient time for the synchronous chat room elements of the activity, you can have learners contribute their one-sentence descriptions in an asynchronous forum.

Websites About Myself

Activity Summary

Learner introductions at the beginning of an online course don't have to be limited to the familiar "name, hometown, and job." The Websites About Myself activity gives learners the opportunity to use the Web to illustrate their interests, backgrounds, and/or experiences as a tool for getting to know their peers.

Goals

- Learners will use the Web as a tool for illustrating their backgrounds, interests, and/or experiences
- Learners will be comfortable interacting with other learners throughout the remainder of the course

Collaborative Learning

Large groups (all learners in a course)

Recommended e-Learning Experience

Learner—Novice
Facilitator—Novice

Mode

Asynchronous

Time Required

Three to five days (once-a-day minimum learner participation)

Materials

- Facilitator and learner access to an online asynchronous discussion board
- Facilitator and learner access to email

Preparation

Create a forum in the course's asynchronous discussion board.

Process

1. Email the learners in the course with the instructions for the activity. Require that each learner post to the discussion forum the URLs (Web addresses) of at least three websites that they believe illustrate their interests, background, and/or experiences. These could include links to their personal websites, the website of a favorite sports team, a website that describes a hobby, or even the website for a company/division. Each learner should include a short description in his or her posting of why he or she selected that particular website to include in his or her introduction.

   Here are some examples:

   - "I'm a little bit of what you would call an NPR junkie and heard about this project on one of their shows. It is a program where high school students in New York City can learn the skills of making radio news and then actually have some of their projects played on NPR. Take a listen to some of them; I think that you will be very impressed: <http://www.wnyc.org/radiorookies/>"

- "Last September I moved from Philadelphia, Pennsylvania <http://www.philly.com/> where the high will be 18 degrees today and the low will be 9 to Tampa, Florida <http://www.visittampabay.com/> where it is about 68 today and will be about 56 tonight."

- "This website is about a nationally known wildlife artist who lives in my hometown. A new center for wildlife and art is being built in his name: <http://www.nedsmithcenter.org/>."

2. Post to the discussion forum three websites that illustrate your interests as a model for learners.

3. Encourage learners to review the Websites About Myself activities of their peers and use these as a tool for getting to know one another.

Facilitator Notes

If there is only limited time for an icebreaker in the course, you can use a variation on this activity by having learners each come to a synchronous chat room discussion prepared to share one website with peers. Then in the synchronous discussion each learner is given an opportunity to share his or her website and why he or she selected that particular website to illustrate his or her background, interests, and/or experiences.

10

Who or What Am I?

Activity Summary

As an icebreaker, the Who or What Am I? activity can be an effective exercise for learners to build online relationships with their peers. Based on the familiar icebreaker that is commonly used in the traditional classroom, the online version uses Internet technologies to supplement questions with websites and other resources.

Goals

- Learners will interact online in order to meet other learners in the course
- Learners will work with their peers to identify the person or object that was assigned to other learners in the course
- Learners will build skills for interacting with other learners in the course

Collaborative Learning

Medium groups (8 to 15 learners)

Recommended e-Learning Experience

Learner—Novice
Facilitator—Novice

Mode

Asynchronous

Time Required

Two to three days (once-a-day minimum learner participation)

Materials

- Facilitator and learner access to an online asynchronous discussion board
- Facilitator and learner access to email

Preparation

1. Identify one course-related historical person or commonly used item for each learner in the course (for example, in a science course with five learners you could choose Einstein, Newton, funnel, thermometer, and beaker; or in a computer course you could choose hard drive, floppy disk, CD-ROM, Bill Gates, Charles Babbage).
2. Establish groups of eight to fifteen learners each.
3. Create a forum in the course's asynchronous discussion board for each group.

Process

1. Email individual learners with the instructions for the activity and assign them one course-related historical person or commonly used item. For example, instructions for the activity could be worded as follows:

"For the Who or What Am I? activity, each participant in the course has been assigned a course-related historical person or commonly used item (for example, if this were a physics course, an historical figure could be Einstein, or if this were a chemistry course a commonly used item could be a petri dish). Your assigned person or item is [insert person or item], and your goal is to determine the assigned person or items for all of the people in your group before they complete their lists. You should use your group's forum in the course's discussion board to ask questions and attempt to determine the historical person or commonly used item assigned to other members of your group. Here are a few rules that you must follow:

- The subject line of the postings in the discussion forum should include the name of the peer you are asking for information from.

- You can only post questions to a specific learner (for example, 'Amanda, did you live in the 20th century?').

- You cannot use any of the individuals or items listed in the activity in asking or answering questions (for example, you can't ask, 'Rose, are you Newton?' or 'Roger, are you a microscope?').

- You cannot use email or instant messengers to ask additional questions.

- As a contest to determine who can correctly match learners with their assigned peers or objects first, you will want to ask questions that may help you determine the match without other learners also identifying the match.

- Your responses may only include:

  Yes—You are sure about your answer of Yes.

  No—You are sure about your answer of No.

  Irrelevant—The question does not apply to your object.

  Probably—You are not sure but you think the answer might be Yes.

  Doubtful—You are not sure but you think the answer might be No.

  Sometimes—Sometimes Yes, sometimes No.

  Usually—Most of the time, the answer would be Yes.

  Rarely—Most of the time, the answer would be No.

  Unknown—You are unsure of how the question relates or you don't know.

- When you believe that you can correctly identify all of the learners in your group with their person or object, then you should email that lists to the facilitator."

2. Post to the discussion board a copy of the activity instructions.

3. Post to the discussion board (a) a list, in random order, of all the historical people or commonly used items that were assigned and (b) a separate list of learners in each group.

4. Have learners use the discussion forum to ask questions and provide answers.

5. When learners believe that they have correctly matched all other members of their group with the assigned historical people or commonly used items, have them email you a complete list.

6. Check the lists submitted to you, and verify when the first learner has correctly matched all of the learners in his or her group with the assigned historical people or commonly used items.

7. End the activity for each group when the first learner correctly matches all learners, and post a copy of the correct answers to the discussion forum.

Facilitator Notes

- You may also want to use a synchronous chat room to facilitate the Who or What Am I? activity in courses where learners will be using synchronous communications throughout the course. This will provide learners with an opportunity to have informal synchronous chats as a way of getting to know one another before formal course discussions are held in the chat room.

- Another variation of the Who or What Am I? activity is the 20 Questions activity (see Activity 62).

11

....

Before, During, and After

Activity Summary

The Before, During, and After activity is a useful technique for understanding what learners bring to a course (that is, pre-existing knowledge and skills), assessing what learners want to accomplish during the course, and identifying how learners will determine whether or not the course has been successful for them.* As a pre-course exercise or icebreaker, this activity can provide you with valuable information for designing and facilitating a course that is both engaging and useful to learners.

Goals

- Learners will assess their current knowledge and skills related to the course content
- Learners will reflect on their expectations for the course
- Learners will identify what criteria they will use in determining whether the course has been successful for them or not
- Learners will share their backgrounds and expectations with both the course facilitator and their peers

Collaborative Learning

Large groups (all learners in a course)

*Based in part on DeBono (1994).

Recommended e-Learning Experience
Learner—Novice
Facilitator—Novice

Mode
Asynchronous

Time Required
Two to three days

Materials
- Facilitator and learner access to an online asynchronous discussion board
- Facilitator and learner access to email

Preparation
Create a forum in the course's asynchronous discussion board for the activity.

Process
1. Email each learner in the course with instructions for the activity. Require learners to post to the discussion forum their responses to the following questions:
   - What skills and/or knowledge related to the course topic do you have at this time?
   - What do you want to learn during this course?
   - How will you determine whether this course has been successful for you?

2. Have each learner post his or her responses to the three questions in the discussion forum.

3. Review and reply to the posted responses of learners in the course, highlighting how the course will meet their goals as well as providing clarification on course objectives and course limitations.

4. Encourage learners to review the postings of their peers.

Facilitator Notes

The activity can also be done with collaborative groups of three to five learners, with each group providing a group response to each question.

12

Who Are We?*

Activity Summary

The Who Are We? activity offers a unique icebreaker to learners in an online course. By engaging all of the learners in the development of a single statement that represents the group identity, this activity can be used to develop an online community within almost any course.

Goals

- Learners will post one- to three-word descriptors of themselves
- Learners will build a composite description of the learners in the course
- Learners will review descriptors provided by their peers in order to identify similar interests

Collaborative Learning

Large groups (all learners in a course)

Recommended e-Learning Experience

Learner—Novice
Facilitator—Novice

*Developed in collaboration with Steve Sugar.

Mode
Synchronous

Time Required
20 to 30 minutes

Materials
- Facilitator and learner access to a synchronous chat room
- Facilitator and learner access to email

Preparation
1. Establish a date and time when the most learners from the course will be available to participate in a synchronous chat room discussion. Depending on the location and schedules of learners, it may be necessary to plan for two or more meetings.
2. Identify a synchronous chat room for the activity. Most online course delivery tools (for example, Blackboard®, WebCT®, LearningSpace®) offer multiple chat rooms that can be used simultaneously for group activities or alone for whole-class activities. From the available chat rooms select a specific chat room (for example, chat room one or chat room A) for the activity.
3. Develop an ordered list of learners in the course (for example, alphabetical, reverse-alphabetical, by location, by time zone).
4. Email learners in the course with the date and time for the synchronous activity. Include with the email the ordered list of learners in the course.

Process

1. Post to the chat room instructions that each learner will be posting a one- to three-word description of himself or herself in the order of the list that you provided.

2. Post to the chat room the introductory statement "We are a. . ."

3. Have the first learner on the list post his or her personal one- to three-word description (for example, runner, teacher, mother, father, crossword puzzler, artist).

4. Then ask the next person on the list to post, and so on through the list.

5. Ask learners to note any peers who have interests similar to their own.

6. When each learner has had an opportunity to post at least one description, you can end the activity or continue for a second round.

Facilitator Notes

To expand the Who Are We? activity, you can identify three to four major categories of descriptors used during the activity (for example, teacher, engineer, parent). After the activity, create forums in the course's asynchronous discussion board for each category and then encourage learners to discuss their similar interests in these forums.

13

What's My Time?

Activity Summary

As an introduction or icebreaker, the What's My Time? activity can be used to engage online learners in discussions with their peers who are living in different time zones around the world. This activity works best for online courses with learners who are located in various time zones, thereby illustrating the challenges and opportunities of synchronous online communications.

Goals

- Learners will identify the time zones in which their online peers are living
- Learners will recognize the challenges and opportunities of communicating with online peers around the world
- Learners will develop skills for effectively communicating online with their peers

Collaborative Learning

Large groups (all learners in a course)

Recommended e-Learning Experience

Learner—Novice
Facilitator—Novice

Mode

Synchronous

Time Required

30 to 40 minutes

Materials

- Facilitator and learner access to a synchronous chat room
- Facilitator and learner access to email

Preparation

1. Identify a synchronous chat room for the activity. Most online course delivery tools (for example, Blackboard®, WebCT®, LearningSpace®) offer multiple chat rooms that can be used simultaneously for group activities or alone for whole-class activities. From the available chat rooms select a specific chat room (for example, chat room one or chat room A) for the activity.

2. Establish a date and time when the most learners from the course will be available to participate in a synchronous chat room discussion.

3. Develop an ordered list of learners in the course (for example, alphabetical or reverse-alphabetical).

Process

1. Email learners in the course with the date and time for the synchronous activity. Include in the email the ordered list of learners.

2. Have the first learner on the list post his or her current location to the chat room (for example, Madrid, Tokyo, Los Angeles).

3. Have other learners in the course post their estimate of what time it would be in the location of the first learner.

4. Have the first learner post when a peer has correctly identified the current time in his or her location.

5. Continue the activity until all learners have had the opportunity to post their locations.

Facilitator Notes

As an alternative, you can transform the activity to "Where Am I?" by having learners post their current time and having their peers attempt to guess their locations based on places within the time zone. For this variation, you may wish to send learners to a website that includes a world map with time zones (for example, <http://www.worldtimezone.com/>) and encourage learners to indicate when their peers have guessed cities that are close to their locations.

Section Three
e-Learning Skills

THE ONLINE CLASSROOM is a new learning environment for learners and instructors alike; and while many participants in your online courses will have been very successful in the traditional training classroom, the e-learning environment offers an array of obstacles and opportunities that learners must attend to in order to continue their success. The activities included in this section focus on helping learners identify and develop the necessary proficiencies for online success.

Success in e-learning requires the integration of new strategies for effectively using online technologies in conjunction with a variety of traditional study skills. As a result, e-learners should both adapt old skills and habits from the traditional classroom for use in the online classroom and acquire new e-learning skills and habits for the online classroom. From applying effective note-taking techniques to establishing reasonable expectations, the activities included in this section can help participants in your courses develop effective e-learning strategies and skills.

e-Learning Study Skills

Activity Summary

While many of the study skills and habits developed for traditional classroom training are useful for online learners, the e-Learning Study Skills activity extends those skills and develops several new ones that will help e-learners to effectively and efficiently learn in the online environment.

Goals

- Learners will adapt study habits developed for the traditional classroom to their online learning
- Learners will adopt new study skills necessary for success in e-learning
- Learners will reflect on what learning strategies will be useful in ensuring their success in the online course

Collaborative Learning

Small groups (3 to 5 learners)

Recommended e-Learning Experience

Learner—Novice
Facilitator—Novice

Mode

Asynchronous

Time Required

Three to five days (once-a-day minimum learner participation)

Materials

- Facilitator and learner access to an online asynchronous discussion board.
- Facilitator and learner access to the World Wide Web

Preparation

1. Assign learners to groups of three to five learners.
2. For each group of learners, select one or more of the following online technologies (giving priority to those used in the current online course):
   - Online real-time chats
   - Online discussion boards
   - Email
   - Listservs
   - Online group projects
   - Online exams
   - Online presentations
   - Online readings
   - Online (electronic) portfolios
   - Turning in assignments online
   - Online whiteboards
   - Online research (or e-research)
3. Create a Study Skills Worksheet for each online technology selected for the activity (or use the one provided with this activity).
4. Create a forum for each group in the course's asynchronous discussion board.

Process

1. Email each group a list of their group members, their assigned online technologies, and a copy of the Study Skills Worksheet.

2. Have learners use email and/or the course's asynchronous discussion board to collaboratively complete the Study Skills Worksheet for the assigned technologies.

3. One learner from each group should post the group's completed Study Skills Worksheet in the designated forum for the activity.

4. Encourage learners to review the posted worksheets of all groups.

Facilitator Notes

- In addition to the online technologies (for example, online chat, online tests, e-research) being used in the current e-learning course, online technologies that learners may use in future courses can also be assigned to groups. This is especially helpful in large courses where group sizes may grow beyond three to five learners.

- More than one group can be assigned to an online technology, giving you the option to have two or three groups each identifying study skills for the use of the same online technology.

Study Skills Worksheet

Instructions: As a group, complete the form below with study skills recommendations for the specific online technology your group has been assigned. For each stage of the online course-work (before, during, after), your group should identify at least three traditional study skills and three new study skills that can improve your learning in this course. When your group has completed the worksheet, post one copy of the worksheet (with the names of all group members) to the identified area of the discussion board.

Assigned technology: _____

Before Using the Online Technology	
Traditional Study Skills	*New Study Skills*
(for example, Review participation rules and guidelines.)	(for example, Check to see if the technology is working.)

| During Use of the Online Technology ||
Traditional Study Skills	**New Study Skills**
(for example, Let other learners complete their statement before starting your reply.)	(for example, Copy and paste postings from Microsoft Word in order to use the spell-check feature.)

| After Using the Online Technology ||
Traditional Study Skills	**New Study Skills**
(for example, Review your notes from the discussion.)	(for example, Determine whether a log or transcript of the discussion was kept electronically and, if so, save a copy of the transcript to your computer—you may be able to simply copy and paste this.)

e-Learning Readiness Self-Assessment

Activity Summary

Self-assessments are a tool that learners can use in developing the learning skills and study habits for online success. The e-Learning Readiness Self-Assessment activity will provide learners with individual feedback on their readiness to be successful in an online course and give them the opportunity to discuss strategies for improving their readiness with their peers.

Goals

- Learners will self-assess their strengths and weaknesses in preparation for success in the online course
- Learners will identify e-learning strategies that may improve their ability to learn in the online classroom
- Learners will apply one or more strategies for improving their readiness for online learning

Collaborative Learning

Individual and small groups (3 to 5 learners)

Recommended e-Learning Experience

Learner—Novice
Facilitator—Novice

Mode
Asynchronous

Time Required
One day (once-a-day minimum learner participation)

Materials
- Facilitator and learner access to email
- Facilitator and learner access to Adobe PDF Reader
- Facilitator and learner access to an online asynchronous discussion board

Preparation
Create a forum in the course's asynchronous discussion board for the activity.

Process
1. Email each learner a copy of the e-Learning Readiness Self-Assessment and the Scoring and Interpretation Sheet.
2. Have each learner complete the self-assessment.
3. Have each learner complete a Scoring and Interpretation Sheet.
4. Based on their self-assessment score and interpretation, instruct learners to discuss the implications of the results on their current and future study habits for the course.
5. Participate in the asynchronous discussion, offering learners a variety of suggestions about how they can be better prepared for success in this and their other online courses.

Facilitator Notes

- The following are examples of questions that you may want to use to guide learner discussions following completion of the self-assessment: "Without giving your scores from any particular area of the self-assessment, which areas did you identify as those in which you could use some additional study strategies or other preparation?" or "Based on your overall score from the self-assessment, what specific strategies are you going to employ during this course to improve your readiness?"

- Instead of having individual learners complete the self-assessment, learners may also use the self-assessment as a tool for stimulating group discussion on topics related to what it takes to be successful in the current and future online courses.

e-Learning Readiness Self-Assessment*

Instructions: For each item below, indicate your agreement with the statement by circling the corresponding value. For each category of statements, calculate your average response by dividing the total value of your responses by the number of items. When you have indicated your response for each item, complete the interpretation table provided at the end of the self-assessment.

1 = Strongly Disagree
2 = Somewhat Disagree
3 = Not Sure
4 = Somewhat Agree
5 = Strongly Agree

Technology Access	I have access to a computer with an Internet connection.	1 2 3 4 5
	I have access to a fairly new computer (enough RAM, speakers, CD-ROM, etc.).	1 2 3 4 5
	I have access to a computer with adequate software (Microsoft Word, Adobe Acrobat, etc.).	1 2 3 4 5
	Average response (total ÷ 3)	

*Used with permission, Watkins and Corry, 2005. Funding for research regarding the internal validity of self-assessment was provided through a grant from the International Society of Performance Improvement.

e-Learning Readiness Self-Assessment *(continued)*

Technology Relationship Skills	I have the basic skills to operate a computer (saving files, creating folders, etc.).	1 2 3 4 5
	I have the basic skills for finding my way around the Internet (using search engines, entering passwords, etc.).	1 2 3 4 5
	I can send an email with a file attached.	1 2 3 4 5
	I think that I would be comfortable using a computer several times a week to participate in a course.	1 2 3 4 5
	I think that I would be able to communicate effectively with others using online technologies (email, chat, etc.).	1 2 3 4 5
	I think that I would be able to express myself clearly through my writing (mood, emotions, humor, etc.).	1 2 3 4 5
	I think that I would be able to use online tools (email, chat, etc.) to work on assignments with learners who are in different time zones.	1 2 3 4 5
	I think that I would be able to schedule time to provide timely responses to other learners and/or the instructor.	1 2 3 4 5
	I think that I would be able to ask questions and make comments in clear writing.	1 2 3 4 5
	Average response (total ÷ 9)	

Motivation	I think that I would be able to remain motivated even though the instructor is not online at all times.	1 2 3 4 5
	I think that I would be able to complete my work even when there are online distractions (friends sending emails, websites to surf, etc.).	1 2 3 4 5
	I think that I would be able to complete my work, even when there are distractions in my home (television, children, and such).	1 2 3 4 5
	Average response (total ÷ 3)	

Online Video/Audio	I think that I would be able to relate the content of short video clips (1 to 3 minutes typically) to the information I have read online or in books.	1 2 3 4 5
	I think that I would be able to take notes while watching a video on the computer.	1 2 3 4 5
	I think that I would be able to understand course-related information when it's presented in video format.	1 2 3 4 5
	Average response (total ÷ 3)	

Internet Discussions	I think that I would be able to carry on a conversation with others using the Internet (Internet chat, instant messenger, etc.).	1 2 3 4 5
	I think that I would be comfortable having several discussions taking place in the same online chat, even though I may not be participating in all of them.	1 2 3 4 5
	I think that I would be able to follow along with an online conversation (Internet chat, instant messenger, etc.) while typing.	1 2 3 4 5
	Average response (total ÷ 3)	

Success Factors	Regular contact with the instructor is important to my success in online coursework.	1 2 3 4 5
	Quick technical and administrative support is important to my success in online coursework.	1 2 3 4 5
	Frequent participation throughout the learning process is important to my success in online coursework.	1 2 3 4 5
	I feel that prior experiences with online technologies (email, Internet chat, online readings, etc.) are important to my success with an online course.	1 2 3 4 5
	The ability to immediately apply course materials is important to my success with online courses.	1 2 3 4 5
	Average response (total ÷ 5)	

After completing the e-Learning Readiness Self-Assessment, review the Scoring and Interpretation Sheet.

e-Learning Readiness Self-Assessment Scoring and Interpretation Sheet

As you completed the e-Learning Readiness Self-Assessment, you should have calculated your average response for each section as you went. This is calculated by dividing the total (the sum) of each section by the number of items included in the section. Enter these averages in the table below:

Your Score	Section of Self-Assessment
	Technology Access
	Technology Relationship Skills
	Motivation
	Online Video/Audio
	Internet Discussions
	Success Factors

If your average score in any area was a 3 or below, please review the following recommendations.

Technology Access

Without adequate access to the technology required in an online course, completing course assignments and engaging with other learners in the course can be challenging. If you have limited access to technology, you should examine alternative resources (such as public libraries, Internet cafes, or local schools) and establish a technology contingency plan just in case you have to complete an online assignment quickly if your technology fails. In addition, contact your instructor at the beginning of the course to verify which software and hardware will be required and what technology resources are provided.

Technology Relationship Skills

Developing positive online relationships is central to an interactive online course. If your scores in this area were low, you will likely want to develop some strategies for addressing those concerns early in the course (for example, making a good first impression online, adding personal touches to online messages, developing online study groups, staying organized and on schedule). Each of the skills that you develop can be helpful in creating a positive online environment where you can work effectively with your peers.

Motivation

Staying motivated is challenging in almost any course, online or in the classroom. For those learners who have not established good study habits and positive support systems, staying motivated can be even more challenging. Identify friends, family, and peers who can provide you with the motivational support that you may require in completing current and future courses. In addition, try to identify those learners in the course with a positive attitude; their positive outlook can be much more useful to you as the course goes on than the negative attitudes that some learners may bring to every online conversation.

Online Audio/Video

If your course utilizes streaming audio or video, then having the necessary study skills to be successful with this technology is essential. If you scored low in this area, and your course facilitator plans to use the technology, you should practice using the technology, taking notes, and studying from the audio/video before your first lesson using the technology. You don't want to waste time or miss any essential points because you didn't develop good study habits for the times when these technologies were in use (just as you wouldn't want to miss taking notes in a traditional lecture because you weren't prepared).

Internet Discussions

Most of the interactions that you will have with your facilitator and peers in an online course will be through Internet discussions (email, asynchronous discussion boards, synchronous chats, and so on). You should develop useful skills for effectively communicating through each type of technical media used in your online course. Have strategies for getting your point across, gaining the attention of others, archiving the conversation, discussing challenging topics without offending other learners, and so forth.

Success Factors

Many factors lead to success in online courses. Your individual study preferences, expectations, and previous experiences will all play a role in your success in current and future online courses. If you have concerns in any of these areas, you should discuss those with your facilitator before committing to a course.

e-Learning Expectations

Activity Summary

The preconceived expectations and assumptions that learners have about e-learning can often define their participation and their success in an online course. As an alternative to these often-uninformed expectations, you can use the e-Learning Expectations activity to clarify and correct any misconceptions learners may have regarding the current online course.

Goals

- Learners will have clear and accurate expectations about what to expect in the current online course
- Learners will be involved in the process of clarifying the expectations established by the facilitator

Collaborative Learning

Large groups (all learners in a course, or groups of 20 to 25)

Recommended e-Learning Experience

Learner—Novice
Facilitator—Novice

Mode

Asynchronous

Time Required

Two to three days (once-a-day minimum learner participation)

Materials

Facilitator and learner access to an online asynchronous discussion board

Preparation

1. Create five to ten forums in the course's asynchronous discussion board.

2. Post in each forum a common assumption or expectation that learners often have regarding e-learning in general or the specific course you are teaching. For example, below are several misconceptions that learners often have regarding online courses:

   - Online courses require less time than traditional classroom courses.

   - Because you would not go to a traditional course every day, you only have to participate in an online course once a week.

   - Online facilitators are always online.

   - Online courses are only for self-directed learners.

   - Making friends in online courses is very difficult.

   - Little feedback is given in online course assignments and activities.

   - Online courses don't require your participation; you can read and be successful.

   - If you don't like to talk in class, then online courses are better for you.

- Online materials are always available when you want them.
- Online courses are just like mail-based correspondence courses, except they use the Internet.

Process

1. Have learners read and react to each of the assumptions and misconceptions. In their posted responses they should give examples of assumptions they have regarding e-learning, describe consequences of misconceptions, and provide online resources (URLs) that give strategies for effective learning online.

2. Clarify any continuing misconceptions that may be apparent based on the responses of the learners.

Facilitator Notes

- Online survey or polling tools can also be used to facilitate this activity if you turn the assumptions or misconceptions into true/false questions.

- As another variation to the activity you can have learners in the course post additional expectations or assumptions they have regarding the course. Other learners can then respond to each of the expectations, and you can clarify any misconceptions they may have.

17

Learning Styles and Study Habits

Activity Summary

Identifying preferred learning styles can help online learners prepare for success in their courses by guiding their study habits and helping them to understand how other learners in the course may benefit from online materials and activities in different ways. The Learning Styles and Study Habits activity will assist learners in identifying their preferences and discussing what variations in their study skills will be most useful in an online course.

Goals

- Learners will identify their preferred learning styles
- Learners will participate in asynchronous discussions with their peers about how to vary their study habits based on their preferred learning styles
- Learners will build online relationships with other learners in the course

Collaborative Learning

Large groups (all learners in a course)

Recommended e-Learning Experience

Learner—Novice
Facilitator—Novice

Mode

Asynchronous

Time Required

Three to five days (once-a-day minimum learner participation)

Materials

- Facilitator and learner access to an online asynchronous discussion board
- Facilitator and learner access to Adobe Reader

Preparation

1. Create three forums in the course's asynchronous discussion board.

2. Post a learning style preference as the topic for each discussion forum (visual, auditory, and tactile/kinesthetic). To begin the discussion in each forum, you can use questions like the following:

   "Subject: Primary Learning Style Is Visual
   "As a learner who prefers visual elements in his or her instruction, what study skills do you believe are most useful in the online course environment? For example, drawing pictures or mind-maps as you read online materials, paying special attention to the images or animated graphics, and/or envisioning the topic in your thoughts."

"Subject: Primary Learning Style Is Auditory

"As a learner who prefers auditory elements in his or her instruction, what study skills do you believe are most useful in the online course environment? For example, developing an internal conversation between you and the text, reading aloud, and/or discussing the topic in verbal conversation with a peer, family member, or colleague at work."

"Subject: Primary Learning Style Is Tactile/Kinesthetic

"As a learner who prefers tactile/kinesthetic elements in his or her instruction, what study skills do you believe are most useful in the online course environment? For example, taking careful notes while reading online material, using a pencil or highlighter to mark your notes, using an online highlighter (for example, with PDF files or Microsoft Word documents), and/or keeping an online journal."

3. Email each learner in the course a copy of the Learning Styles Inventory. Include in the email instructions to participate in the asynchronous discussions related to their preferred learning style in the course's asynchronous discussion board.

Process

1. Have learners complete the Learning Styles Inventory.

2. Have learners discuss the implications their preferred learning style has on their study habits in an online course. Learners should only participate in the discussion forum for the learning style they selected using the inventory.

3. Participate in all three of the learning styles discussions, offering tips and suggestions for becoming a more effective e-learner.

Facilitator Notes

After individual learners complete the Learning Styles Inventory, three synchronous chat rooms can be created for real-time discussions of the related variations in study skills that may be appropriate for the preferred learning style. By using synchronous chat rooms, you can reduce the time required for the Learning Styles and Study Habits activity to just one hour.

Learning Styles Inventory*

Learning styles refer to the ways you prefer to approach new information. Each of us learns and processes information in our own special ways, although we share some learning patterns, preferences, and approaches. Knowing your preferred style also can help you to realize that other people may approach the same situation in a different way from your own.

Take a few minutes to complete the following questionnaire to assess your preferred learning style. Begin by reading the words in the left-hand column. Of the three responses to the right, check the one that best characterizes you, answering as honestly as possible with the description that applies to you right now. Count the number of checked items and write your total at the bottom of each column. The questions you select will offer insight about how you prefer to learn.

1. *Concentrating*	❏ Does seeing untidiness or movement distract you? Do you notice things in your visual field that other people don't?	❏ Are you distracted by sounds or noises? Do you prefer to manage the amount and the type of noise around you?	❏ Are you distracted by activity around you? Do you shut out conversations and go inside yourself?
2. *Visualizing*	❏ Do you see vivid, detailed pictures in your thoughts?	❏ Do you think in sounds and voices?	❏ Do the images you see in your thoughts involve movement?

Totals	Visual: _____	Auditory: _____	Tactile/ Kinesthetic: _____

*Used with permission from Conner, 2004.

3. *Talking*	❏ Do you dislike listening for a long time? Do you often use words such as see, picture, and imagine?	❏ Do you enjoy listening? (Or maybe you're impatient to talk?) Do you often use words such as say, hear, tune, and think?	❏ Do you like to gesture and use expressive movements? Do you often use words such as feel, touch, and hold?
4. *Contacting People*	❏ Do you prefer direct, face-to-face, personal meetings?	❏ Do you prefer the telephone for intense conversations?	❏ Do you prefer to talk while walking or participating in an activity?
5. *Meeting Someone Again*	❏ Do you forget names but remember faces? Can you usually remember where you met someone	❏ Do you tend to remember people's names? Can you usually remember what you talked about?	❏ Do you tend to remember what you did together? Can you almost feel your time together?
6. *Relaxing*	❏ Do you prefer to watch TV, see a play, go to a movie?	❏ Do you prefer to listen to the radio, play music, read, talk with a friend?	❏ Do you prefer to play sports, knit, build something with your hands?
7. *Reading*	❏ Do you like descriptive scenes? Do you pause to imagine the action?	❏ Do you enjoy the dialogue most? Can you "hear" the characters talk?	❏ Do you prefer action stories? (Or maybe don't even enjoy reading for pleasure?)

Totals   Visual: _____   Auditory: _____   Tactile/
                                                                          Kinesthetic: _____

8. Spelling	❑ Do you try to see the word in your mind? Do you imagine what it would look like on paper?	❑ Do you use a phonetic approach to sound out the word? Do you hear it in your thoughts or say it aloud?	❑ Do you write down the word to find out if it feels right? Maybe you run your finger over it or type it out?
9. Doing Something New at Work	❑ Do you like to see demonstrations, diagrams, and flow charts? Do you seek out pictures or diagrams?	❑ Do you find verbal and written instructions helpful? Do you like talking it over? Do you ask a neighbor?	❑ Do you prefer to jump right in and try it? Do you keep trying? Do you try different ways?
10. Putting Something Together	❑ Do you look at the picture and then, maybe, read the directions?	❑ Do you like reading or talking with someone about it? Do you find yourself talking aloud as you work?	❑ Do you usually ignore the directions and figure it out as you go along?
11. Interpreting Mood	❑ Do you primarily look at facial expressions?	❑ Do you listen to the tone of voice?	❑ Do you watch for body language?
12. Teaching People	❑ Do you prefer to show them?	❑ Do you prefer to tell them? Write it out?	❑ Do you demonstrate how it's done? Ask them to try it?

Totals	Visual: _____	Auditory: _____	Tactile/ Kinesthetic: _____

The column with the highest total represents your primary preference as a processing style. The column with the second-most choices is your secondary style. If there are two learning styles that have the same score, then you should select the one that you believe best illustrates your learning style preference.

Your primary learning style: _____

Your secondary learning style: _____

When you have completed and scored the Learning Styles Inventory, you should go the course's asynchronous discussion board to participate in the discussions related to your primary learning style.

18

25-15-5 Goal Development

Activity Summary

Two of the skills that are vital to success of e-learners are setting goals and learning to communicate efficiently. The 25–15–5 Goal Development activity supports online learners in establishing clear goals and communicating them effectively online.

Goals

- Learners will identify and communicate their goals for the online course
- Learners will build skills necessary for efficiently communicating with their peers using online tools

Collaborative Learning

Large groups (all learners in a course)

Recommended e-Learning Experience

Learner—Novice
Facilitator—Novice

Mode

Asynchronous

Time Required

Three to five days (once-a-day minimum learner participation)

Materials

- Facilitator and learner access to an online asynchronous discussion board
- Facilitator and learner access to email

Preparation

1. Create a forum in the course's asynchronous discussion board.

2. Email learners informing them that they will be required to participate in the activity at least once a day for each of the next three days.

Process

Day One

1. Email the learners in the course instructing them to compose a twenty-five-word personal goal statement for the course. This statement, identifying what they want to achieve in the course, should be precisely twenty-five words long (which may take some editing and refinement on the part of the learners).

2. Have learners post their goal statements in the discussion forum.

3. Request that learners neither respond nor reply to the goal statements contributed by their peers.

Day Two

4. Email the learners in the course instructing them to revise their personal goal statements from Day One. The revised goal statement should now be precisely fifteen words long (which may take some editing and refinement on the part of the learners).

5. Have learners respond (or reply) to their posted goal statements from the day before with their fifteen-word goal statements.

6. Request that learners neither respond nor reply to the goal statements contributed by their peers.

Day Three
7. Email the learners in the course instructing them to revise their personal goal statements from Day Two. The revised goal statements should now be precisely five words long (which may take some editing and refinement on the part of the learners).

8. Have learners respond (or reply) to their posted goal statements from the day before with their five-word goal statements.

Day Four
9. Have learners review and comment on the posted goal statements of their peers in the course.

Facilitator Notes

- The 25–25–5 Goal Development activity can also be done using a synchronous chat room, although facilitating the discussion can be challenging.

- Other variations of the activity can include having learners develop twenty-five-word, fifteen-word, and five-word descriptions of concepts or ideas related to the course content, rather than their goals for the course. These activities can help learners to formulate and clearly communicate key concepts and ideas that they are learning about in the course.

19

Lessons Learned the Hard Way

Activity Summary

Learners come to online courses with a history of positive and negative experiences both as students and as users of technology. The Lessons Learned the Hard Way activity will utilize these experiences to build online relationships as well as to guide other learners in avoiding many of the pitfalls of online courses.

Goals

- Learners will share the lessons they have learned from their positive and negative experiences as students (online or traditional)
- Learners will share the lessons they have learned from their positive and negative experiences as users of technology
- Learners will build on relationships with their peers in the course

Collaborative Learning

Medium groups (8 to 15 learners)

Recommended e-Learning Experience

Learner—Novice
Facilitator—Novice

Mode
Asynchronous

Time Required
Two to three days (once-a-day minimum learner participation)

Materials
- Facilitator and learner access to an online asynchronous discussion board
- Facilitator and learner access to email

Preparation
Create a forum in the course's asynchronous discussion board.

Process
1. Email the learners in the course the instructions for the activity. Require learners to post at least one lesson they have "learned the hard way" either as a student (online or traditional) or as a user of technology. Each lesson should include (a) background information or context, (b) what happened, (c) what they now do differently, and (d) a subject line that describes the lesson learned.

   For example:

   "Subject: Keeping Up in Real-Time Chats
   "As an online learner I discovered the hard way that you should write out in Microsoft Word what you want to say in real-time chat before the synchronous discussion begins. It was my first online course and I thought that I would just join in the conversation and see what happened.

But with 12+ people all online and chatting at the same time I never had time to write out what I wanted to ask the facilitator before the screen would scroll down and I would miss half the conversation. So now I type out my questions beforehand and cut and paste them into the chat when I am ready. This way I can quickly get my question in and not miss any of the conversation."

"Subject: Technology Contingency Plan
"Having worked as a computer programmer for the past several years I have learned the hard way that you always have to have a technology contingency plan. Computers will invariably have glitches or software problems whenever you have a deadline to meet. As a result, you should also have the support phone numbers readily available and know where you can get computer access other than on your home computer (for example, local library, coffee shop, college computer lab, or a neighbor's house)."

2. Encourage learners to review the postings of their peers and make comments or recommendations based on the experiences of their fellow learners.

Facilitator Notes

If the learners in your course all have prior experience in taking online courses, then you can limit the range of lessons learned to those that they can identify from their last online course experience or even their previous online course experiences with you as the facilitator.

20

Pre-Reading Questions

Activity Summary

Reading online books, articles, papers, and essays requires many of the same comprehension building skills and habits that are necessary for effective reading of paper-based materials. Yet, too often e-learners do not apply the same reading techniques that make them successful in traditional courses when they move to online reading. The Pre-Reading Questions activity is an interactive exercise that you can use to encourage learners to practice this effective strategy for improving reading comprehension.

Goals

- Learners will preview online readings
- Learners will identify questions to be answered from the readings
- Learners will collaborate with their peers in developing pre-reading questions

Collaborative Learning

Large groups (all learners in a course)

Recommended e-Learning Experience

Learner—Novice
Facilitator—Novice

Mode
Asynchronous

Time Required
Two to three days (once-a-day minimum learner participation)

Materials
- Facilitator and learner access to an online asynchronous discussion board
- Facilitator and learner access to email

Preparation
1. Select an online reading assignment (for example, an online article, website, or chapter in an e-book).
2. Create two forums in the course's asynchronous discussion board: one titled "Pre-Reading Questions" and one "Pre-Reading Answers."

Process
1. Email learners with instructions for the activity, letting them know they are to post to the discussion board forum prior to reading the assigned materials.
2. Have learners browse or scan the required online readings for the activity.
3. Have each learner identify three questions that should be answered when reading the assigned materials.
4. Request that learners post their three pre-reading questions to the discussion forum prior to completing their detailed reading of the assigned materials.

5. Encourage learners to review the posted questions of their peers prior to reading.

6. Ask learners to then read the course materials carefully, answering the questions they (and their peers) identified as they read.

7. Have learners post the answers to the pre-reading questions in the second discussion forum.

Facilitator Notes

• As a variation, use this activity with small groups (three to five learners each) to encourage additional collaboration in the development of pre-reading questions.

• You may also want to use this activity even when online readings are not required for the course. Learners can also improve comprehension when reading paper-based materials by developing pre-reading questions.

21

Take Note

Activity Summary

Taking notes while reading online books, articles, postings, emails, and other materials is an essential task for building comprehension. The Take Note activity provides learners with an opportunity to practice using technology for taking notes while reading course materials.

Goals

- Learners will use technology to assist in taking notes while completing online readings
- Learners will collaborate in the development of online note-taking strategies for use in online courses

Collaborative Learning

Small groups (3 to 5 learners each)

Recommended e-Learning Experience

Learner—Novice
Facilitator—Novice

Mode

Asynchronous

Time Required

Three to five days (once-a-day minimum learner participation)

Materials

- Facilitator and learner access to an online asynchronous discussion board
- Learner access to a word processing software application (for example, Microsoft WordPad®, Notepad®, Word®, or Corel WordPerfect®)
- Facilitator and learner access to email

Preparation

1. Identify one or two of the more complex online readings for your online course.
2. Create a forum in the course's asynchronous discussion board for the activity.

Process

1. Email learners with the assigned readings and a description of the activity.
2. Have learners briefly browse or scan the required materials one time through completely, not taking notes but rather gaining an understanding of the main ideas and key issues.
3. Have learners open a word processing program (such as Microsoft WordPad) for taking notes.
4. Have learners read the required materials a second time, this time identifying and taking notes on major topics, subtopics, themes, and key vocabulary terms using the word processing software.
5. Require learners to copy and paste their notes from the readings to the discussion forum.

6. Encourage learners to review the notes taken by peers, comparing their notes and identifying how other learners may have used their notes more effectively to study the course materials.

7. Encourage learners to review the readings a third time in order to verify their understanding of the materials and the accuracy of their notes.

Facilitator Notes

- For learners with more advanced e-learning skills, you may want to require that learners also add a concept (or mind) map to their notes. This map will illustrate the relationships between the review topics discussed in the readings.

- If online readings are in Word, WordPerfect, or Adobe PDF format, then you may also encourage learners to underline, highlight, and/or use the add comments features of these software applications. These can be effective tools for taking notes while reading online materials.

Section Four
Collaboration and Team Building

· ·

INTERACTIVE AND ENGAGING ONLINE EXPERIENCES are often created when instructors incorporate small group activities or team projects into their courses. In much the same way that traditional classroom courses use collaborative activities, online courses can use small group and team tasks to accomplish a variety of learning objectives. In addition, online courses can use collaborative activities as a means of increasing the interactivity among learners in the courses without necessarily involving the instructor in every online conversation.

While many of the e-learning activities included in this book are designed to use collaborative groups, included in this section of the book are a variety of activities designed to help e-learners create the positive group norms and dynamics that are essential to the success of online teams. From assigning team member responsibilities to gaining peer buy-in to group goals, these activities can be used in tandem with other e-learning activities to assist learners who may struggle with the development of effective small group or team relationships in the online classroom.

22

Group Norms

Activity Summary

Interactive online courses that use group tasks and assignments typically require learners to quickly establish group norms using the available online communication tools. The Group Norms activity is intended to facilitate that process for learners, thus allowing them to more quickly move from "forming" and "norming" to "storming" and "performing"(Tuckman, 1965).

Goals

- Learners will identify the necessary norms for an effective online group
- Learners will negotiate preliminary norms for the online working group
- Learners will gain skills in effectively communicating using an online asynchronous discussion board

Collaborative Learning

Small groups (3 to 8 learners)

Recommended e-Learning Experience

Learner—Novice
Facilitator—Novice

Mode

Asynchronous

Time Required

Two to three days (once-a-day minimum learner participation)

Materials

- Learner access to an online asynchronous discussion board
- Facilitator and learner access to email

Preparation

1. Assign learners in the course to collaborative groups of three to eight learners per group.
2. Create a forum in the course's asynchronous discussion board for each group.
3. Post the following list of topics to be discussed within each group's forum.*

- *Establishing Roles:* discussion leader, note taker, liaison with facilitator, etc.
- *Timeliness:* start time, finish time, lateness, and attendance
- *Courtesy:* listening, interruptions, equal participation, dealing with disagreements, respect, empathy, and sharing the workload
- *Decision-Making Process:* How will we make decisions? Reach agreements? How will we show agreement?
- *Workload Assignment:* How will work be assigned? How will conflicts with existing workloads be settled?
- *Setting Priorities:* How will we discharge responsibility for on-time completion and equal distribution?
- *Enforcement of Norms:* How will we make sure the norms are followed?

*Topics based on *Setting Norms for Collaborative Work* (Koppett & Richter,

Process

1. Email learners with the directions for the activity. In the message, include the names and email address for the members of each group. You can use the activity description below as a basis for your email directions:

   "In completing this activity as a group, you will want to identify and establish some agreed-on group norms to facilitate your work. Developing effective group norms for online teams requires that all team members participate in the Group Norms discussion (located in the identified group areas of the course's asynchronous discussion board).

   "The Group Norms activity requires each group member to review the seven areas identified below, in which preliminary norms or rules of etiquette should be agreed on prior to moving forward with any group project. When each of the seven areas has been discussed within your group and at least preliminary norms have been established for the group, one team member should summarize the group's norms in the seven areas within a single posting to the discussion board so that they can later be reviewed (and possibly updated).

   - *Establishing Roles:* discussion leader, note taker, liaison with facilitator, etc.

   - *Timeliness:* start time, finish time, lateness, and attendance

   - *Courtesy:* listening, interruptions, equal participation, dealing with disagreements, respect, empathy, and sharing the workload

- *Decision-Making Process:* How will we make decisions? Reach agreements? How will we show agreement?

- *Workload Assignment:* How will work be assigned? How will conflicts with existing workloads be settled?

- *Setting Priorities:* How will we discharge responsibility for on-time completion and equal distribution?

- *Enforcement of Norms:* How will we make sure the norms are followed?"

2. Have learners participate in discussions related to the group norms.

3. Have one member post to the discussion board the preliminary norms decided on by each group.

4. Review the discussions taking place in each group's asynchronous discussion forum throughout the activity. Encourage learners to review and comment on the norms established by their peer groups.

Facilitator Notes

- The Group Norms activity can also be completed by groups using synchronous chat rooms if that is more appropriate given the characteristics of the online course and learners. Using synchronous chat rooms can reduce the amount of time required for the activity and encourage learners to develop the skills necessary for effective communication in online synchronous chats, although additional e-learning experience is likely required of learners.

- As a variation to the activity, have learners within each group sign a "contract" that identifies the agreed-on norms and rules of etiquette that will be followed in all group activities.

23

Group Member Responsibilities

Activity Summary

Interactive online courses typically require learners to participate in a range of group activities. The Group Member Responsibilities activity can be used to increase the awareness and preparation of learners for the responsibilities they will have as online group members.

Goals

- Learners will identify the primary responsibilities of an effective online group
- Learners will engage in discussions with other learners on the responsibilities they have within online groups
- Learners will be more effective users of online asynchronous discussion boards

Collaborative Learning

Medium groups (8 to 15 learners)

Recommended e-Learning Experience

Learner—Novice
Facilitator—Experienced

Mode

Synchronous

Time Required

60 to 90 minutes

Materials

- Facilitator and learner access to email
- Facilitator and learner access to an online synchronous chat room

Preparation

1. Review, update, and reduce the following list of responsibilities associated with making a positive contribution to the efforts of an online team to ten items that are critical to success in your online course.

Responsibilities of Contributing Group Members*

- Come to online group meetings on time (if synchronous) prepared to contribute to group discussions.
- Maintain your role (e.g., leader, organizer, note taker).
- Keep records of what has been agreed on.
- Try to find common direction in working with others.
- Be a resource for the group.
- Listen to the ideas of others (read the entire posting before commenting).
- Take responsibility for helping the group.
- Make decisions and solve problems, rather than complaining.

*Based in part on Watkins and Corry (2005) and *Group Effectiveness* (1994).

- Speak only for yourself.
- Help evaluate the group effort.
- Self-evaluate your own contributions.
- Keep discussions focused.
- Do not disappear (e.g., stop answering email) without notification.
- Synthesize various contributions.
- Recognize, celebrate, and honor successes.
- Complete the tasks you agree to complete.
- Resist over-analysis of group discussions.
- Follow the group's communication strategy.
- Avoid sarcasm, slang, jargon, and idioms.
- Be careful of miscommunication in online discussions.

2. Identify a synchronous chat room for the activity. Most online course delivery tools (for example, Blackboard®, WebCT®, LearningSpace®) offer multiple chat rooms that can be used simultaneously for group activities or alone for whole-class activities. From the available chat rooms you should select a specific chat room (that is, chat room one or chat room A) for the activity.

3. Establish a date and time when the most learners from the course will be available to participate in a synchronous chat room discussion.

4. Email learners the list of ten responsibilities associated with making a positive contribution to the efforts of an online team, and ask learners to rank the list of responsibilities based on their perceived importance to success in the current online course (10 being the most critical and 1 the least critical). Also include the date and time of the synchronous group discussion.

Process

1. Post the first of the ten responsibilities to the synchronous chat room.

2. Have learners post a ranking for the first responsibility.

3. Add the numbers associated with each ranking provided by learners.

4. Post each of the remaining responsibilities one at a time, allowing learners to post their rankings after each.

5. Provide the results to learners, showing which responsibilities received the highest totals.

6. Lead a discussion on why specific responsibilities were selected and how they can be implemented within the course's online groups.

7. Ask the learners whether they have any additional group member responsibilities that they believe should be added to the list.

Facilitator Notes

- This activity can also be done using online asynchronous discussion boards. The asynchronous variation of this activity should be made available to learners for five to seven days, depending on the requirements of the course for online participation.

- If you have access to online survey or polling software (either within a course management system or using a software application associated with a course webpage) then the activity can be completed within 15 to 20 minutes, including the group discussion.

24

Gaining Buy-In

Activity Summary

Engaging learners in any course requires that participants believe in the importance of the goals, be motivated by the goals, and buy into the value and utility of course objectives. The Gaining Buy-In activity is an introductory tool that can encourage learners to discuss the value of accomplishing course objectives and motivate learners to support the goals of the online course.

Goals

- Learners will encourage each other to accept and support the goals and objectives of the online course
- Learners will be motivated to participate in the online course's activities and assignments
- Learners will work together to define the value in achieving the goals of the course

Collaborative Learning

Large groups (all learners in a course)

Recommended e-Learning Experience

Learner—Novice
Facilitator—Moderate

Mode

Asynchronous

Time Required

Three to five days (once-a-day minimum learner participation)

Materials

- Facilitator and learner access to an online asynchronous discussion board
- Facilitator and learner access to email

Preparation

1. Verify that course goals and objectives are

   - Each expressed in clear and concise statements;
   - Focused on the performance of learners (stating what they will know or be able to do after successfully completing the course, rather than vague statements about what they may "understand" or "appreciate");
   - Aligned with the content of the course; and
   - Linked clearly to the application of the knowledge and skills in the workplace after the course.

2. Create two or more forums in the course's online asynchronous discussion board.

3. Develop an initial question related to course goals and objectives for each forum.

   The following are some sample questions:

   - After successfully accomplishing the objectives of this course, each of you should be prepared to apply the knowledge and skills from the course in your work. How do you anticipate using the knowledge and skills from this course in your work?

- All of the goals and objectives of this course are intended to prepare you for success in your work. Which three do you believe will have the most impact on your ability to be successful?

- Courses are developed in order to provide learners with useful skills and knowledge. Of the goals for this course, identify one that you believe to be the most useful and describe how having that knowledge or skill will be of value to you.

- Envision yourself as a supervisor who really wants an employee to take this course. Choose one of the objectives from the course and explain to the employee why attaining that skill or knowledge is essential to his or her success.

Process

1. Email learners instructions for participation in the activity and include a list of course goals and objectives.

2. Have learners participate in online discussions related to each of the questions you posted in the asynchronous discussion forums.

3. Participate with learners in each discussion forum, providing clarification on objectives, adding ideas for how the knowledge and skills gained through the course can be applied, and ensuring that all learners have a positive and optimistic perception of the course aims.

Facilitator Notes

- The Gaining Buy-In activity can also be used as a small group activity. In this variation you may either provide each group with a different question to respond to in building support for the goals of the course or you may use the same question to start the conversation for each group.

- You may also choose to use the Gaining Buy-In activity with drafts of the course goals and objectives. This allows learners to help create the objectives and provide input to the direction the course will take before the course progresses.

25

Setting Discussion Ground Rules

Activity Summary

Effective online discussions require established ground rules that can be used to facilitate the discussion while at the same time maintain a focus on course-related content. The Setting Discussion Ground Rules activity allows learners to participate in the establishment of guidelines and policies that will be used to manage the online synchronous or asynchronous discussions in the course. This activity is most useful when done prior to another online discussion exercise in a course.

Goals

- Learners will provide input and discussion related to ground rules that will be used to facilitate online course dialogues
- Learners will agree on policies for managing synchronous and/or asynchronous online discussions
- Learners will build online communication skills

Collaborative Learning

Large groups (all learners in a course)

Recommended e-Learning Experience

Learner—Novice
Facilitator—Novice

Mode
Asynchronous

Time Required
Two to three days (once-a-day minimum learner participation)

Materials
- Facilitator and learner access to an online asynchronous discussion board
- Facilitator and learner access to email

Preparation
1. Determine whether the activity is going to focus on the ground rules (that is, policies, guidelines, rules) for learner participation in synchronous chat room, asynchronous discussion board, email discussions, or all three.

2. Create a forum in the course's asynchronous discussion board for the activity.

Process
1. Email learners instructions for the activity. A sample email focused on asynchronous discussion boards is shown below:

To: Course learners

From: Facilitator

Re: Setting discussion ground rules activity

Active participation in online asynchronous discussions can be essential to your success in this course, yet without ground rules for managing the discussions we may have miscommunications, lose focus, or even offend other learners in this course. The goal of this activity is to establish and agree to some basic ground rules or policies that we can use throughout the course to facilitate effective and useful online discussions related to course topics. For example, one ground rule that we may agree to is that all postings to the discussion board will have distinct subject lines that identify the major theme of the postings.

Using the discussion forum created in the course's asynchronous discussion board, over the next three days you should post any policies or norms that you believe would make our use of the online discussion board more effective during the course. You should also review the suggested ground rules provided by other learners and post any statements of support or disagreement that you would like to be taken into consideration. Establishing ground rules for the course's online discussions will be beneficial to all of us throughout the course.

2. Have learners participate in the discussion of ground rules in the forum.

3. Monitor the discussion and offer suggestions based on your experiences in using the synchronous or asynchronous discussion tools available for the course. (See Watkins and Corry [2005] for sample ground rules that can be used in online course discussions as well as additional tips for facilitating an effective synchronous chat room discussion.)

4. End the activity by posting a summary of the ground rules that were agreed on by the learners in the course. If there are additional rules that you typically require, if there were ground rules that produced a great deal of debate, or if you have changes that you would like to make to the rules proposed by the group, you should include those comments in the summary.

Facilitator Notes

- The Setting Discussion Ground Rules activity can be done using a synchronous chat room, although when using this variation you should provide some basic rules (for example, protocols for asking a question, everyone not saying "hello" when they first enter the chat) to facilitate the activity until ground rules are established.

- As a variation you may also want to use online polls or surveys to have learners vote on the ground rules that are proposed during the activity.

26

Playing Roles in a Group

Activity Summary

The Playing Roles in a Group activity is intended to challenge learners to take on roles within a group discussion (for example, idea proposer, disagreer, devil's advocate) that may otherwise have not been characterized by online group members. By requiring learners to take on roles or characters within group activities, you can ensure that discussions are both robust and diverse, and that learners will gain an appreciation for viewpoints that other learners may present in course discussions.

Goals

- Learners will discuss a topic from a viewpoint that may or may not be their own
- Learners will describe alternative viewpoints with other learners who have been in different roles within the discussion
- Learners will be more engaged in the group discussion

Collaborative Learning

Medium groups (10 to 15 learners)

Recommended e-Learning Experience

Learner—Novice
Facilitator—Novice

Mode

Asynchronous

Time Required

Three to five days (once-a-day minimum learner participation)

Materials

- Facilitator and learner access to an online asynchronous discussion board
- Facilitator and learner access to email

Preparation

1. Create groups of ten to fifteen learners each.
2. Create a discussion forum for each group in the course's asynchronous discussion board.
3. Identify a topic or question for discussion during the activity.
4. Assign learners in each group to a role they are to play during the discussion. More than one learner in a group can have the same role, although there should be enough variety in roles to ensure that the group discussion will be engaging to all learners.

   Examples of roles that you may assign learners include idea proposer, supporter, questioner, agreer, nay-sayer, example giver, disagreer, big picture framer, small picture framer, clarifier, tension reliever, discussion leader, devil's advocate, discussion tracker or note taker, online resource finder, conflict negotiator, theme summarizer, moderator, monitor, idea generator, fact supplier, and/or clarifier.

Process

1. Post the topic or question to each group's discussion forum.

2. Email learners instructions for participating in the activity and their assigned roles.

3. Have learners discuss the topic or answer the question you have posted in the forum from the perspectives of the roles that they were assigned.

4. Facilitate the discussion by reminding group members of their assigned roles.

Facilitator Notes

The roles used in this activity can also be used to add diversity to interactions when using other e-learning activities included in this book.

Elaborating on Course Content

MOST ONLINE COURSES can benefit from the addition of e-learning activities that expand or enhance the learners' understanding of course-related content. While individual self-paced courses may have the capacity to accomplish many learning objectives, oftentimes we can reduce the time required for learners to achieve success and improve the quality of the learning experience by introducing activities that engage learners in discussions with other learners or the instructor. These interactive exercises provide learners with an opportunity to question assumptions, challenge attitudes, gain a broader perspective on issues, develop constructive study skills, and/or work with others to build proficiencies related to course concepts or tasks.

The activities described in this section encourage learners to become active participants in discussions that elaborate on course content. Often, these activities are most effective when paired with the most challenging concepts or tasks included in an online course, although many times I find that learners can master the most challenging topics more easily when we have developed constructive online relationships through the introduction of these e-learning activities during our discussions of less demanding concepts or tasks. As a result, there is no single topic in a course that can be distinguished from the others as the ideal mate for the activities included in this section, and I suggest that you try to incorporate the exercises several times throughout your course in order to identify where and when they are most effective for achieving your objectives.

27

Resource Scavenger Hunt

Activity Summary

Web-based scavenger hunts encourage learners to explore various online resources and engage in fact-finding exercises in each website they visit. By challenging learners to locate specific information, the Resource Scavenger Hunt activity guides learners to essential resources while at the same time engaging them in an entertaining course exercise.

Goals

- Learners will identify and locate the online resources they will have available to them during the course
- Learners will search available online resources in order to answer specific questions about the available resources
- Learners will be more effective users of online resources throughout the course

Collaborative Learning

Individual with facilitator feedback

Recommended e-Learning Experience

Learner—Novice
Facilitator—Novice

Mode

Asynchronous

Time Required

30 to 40 minutes for every ten to fifteen items

Materials

- Facilitator and learner access to the World Wide Web
- Facilitator and learner access to email

Preparation

1. Identify websites that will be useful to learners throughout the course (for example, technical support, online articles, professional associations, content-related webpages, course policies).

2. Identify at least one specific fact within each online resource that is beneficial for learners (for example, hours for online technical support, full-text online article, instructions for submitting course assignments).

3. Construct a question related to a specific fact from each website. Some examples follow:

   - The technical support staff for our company provides a variety of services to online learners. List three of the primary services they provide.

   - For the third assignment of this online course, you are to submit a complete process diagram for a needs assessment within your organization. What technologies are to be used to submit this assignment to the instructor?

   - In order to access your email for this course, you must sign up for an account. What email address do you write to when requesting your account?

   - Who is the current president of the XYZ professional association?

- On which webpage will you find the login screen to access the online database of articles published in the XYZ magazine? Please provide the webpage address (URL).

Process

1. Email learners the online scavenger hunt questions.
2. Have learners email you back the answers to the scavenger hunt questions.
3. Provide learners with feedback on their performance.

Facilitator Notes

- Learners can also develop online scavenger hunts for other learners to complete when the goal of the instructional activity is to provide learners with a variety of online resources for completing a task (see activity 31, Learner-Crafted Scavenger Hunts).

- Depending on the complexity of the online scavenger hunt items, it can sometimes be useful to provide clues or starting places for learners to begin their search. For example, you may want to provide the URL at which students can begin their search for technical support services (for example, begin at www.ourcompany.com). Determining whether clues are necessary, or desirable, typically depends on the difficulty of the search and the amount of time allowed for learners to complete the Resource Scavenger Hunt activity.

28

Virtual Tours

Activity Summary

The Virtual Tours activity can be used at most any point of an online course to provide learners with a guided exploration of a website. With a structured tour, you can identify specific functions and resources that are available to learners as well as provide instructions on utilizing a variety of resources available during the course.

Goals

- Learners will be familiar with the structure and organization of the targeted website(s)
- Learners will gain skills for discovering useful information when visiting targeted website(s)

Collaborative Learning

Large groups (up to 25 to 30 learners)

Recommended e-Learning Experience

Learner—Novice
Facilitator—Moderate

Mode

Synchronous (although asynchronous variations can be used, see activity 6, Tour My Favorite Website)

Time Required

60 to 90 minutes (approximately 10 minutes per page within a website)

Materials

- Facilitator and learner access to the World Wide Web
- Facilitator and learner access to Web-sharing software (a feature of many learning management systems, groupware or team software systems, chat rooms, online whiteboards, instant messenger services, as well as function-specific software that can be downloaded)

Preparation

1. Select one or more websites that will be of value to learners during the course. For example, you may want learners to locate and review online journal articles related to the course topic. By initially taking learners on a virtual tour of the available website(s) for accessing the related articles to the course topic, you can provide learners with an illustrated example of how to search for relevant articles, retrieve articles, and then save those articles to their computers for later review.

2. Develop a plan for how the guided tour will proceed (that is, pages to be viewed, order of viewing, time spent at each page, key functions to be illustrated, critical information).

3. Identify available software with Web-sharing capabilities. You may want to contact technical support for assistance in installing and using the Web-sharing features (a feature of many learning management systems, groupware or team software systems, chat rooms, online whiteboards, instant messenger services, as well as function-specific software that can be downloaded).

4. Notify the learners, at least two days in advance, of time and software requirements for the virtual tour. Include the goals of the tour (that is, what knowledge and skills the learners should be paying special attention for during the tour) as well as any suggestions for online etiquette during the tour, such as holding questions for the end of the tour or not doing other work online at the same time).

5. The day before, test the software and websites to be used in the tour.

Process

1. Arrive at the desired online location at least five minutes in advance to verify that all of the technology required for the activity is working properly. If it is not, promptly contact technical support staff and email learners about potential delays in the activity.

2. Welcome learners to the Virtual Tour and provide a short introduction to the website they will tour during the activity.

3. Use the previously created plan and spend enough time on each webpage for learners to review all of the visible material. Add comments to the discussion regarding the unique or critical tools on each webpage.

4. Email learners a list of websites visited during the tour, since they may not have taken accurate notes.

Facilitator Notes

- During a Virtual Tour it is often useful to have learners practice a task that may be done on a webpage (that is, search for an article, complete an online form, identify critical information from the website). Many Web-sharing applications permit learners to "take over" a virtual tour and practice the use of website functions while being directed by the facilitator.

- As a variation, have learners create and guide virtual tours with their peers (see activity 6, Tour My Favorite Website, for an asynchronous variation)

- Many Web-sharing software applications have the capability to record a virtual tour. Recorded tours can be used as an asynchronous activity for learners. If a tour is being recorded, learners should be informed prior to beginning the tour, as it may change their note-taking and question-asking strategies.

29

Telling a Story

Activity Summary

Each of us has a story to tell. The Telling a Story activity creates an environment in an online course where learners can add their stories to the conversation, thus building community, engaging the learners in the course, and improving retention of course materials. As an icebreaker or within the content of the course, this activity can provide learners with the opportunity to tell their stories.

Goals

- Learners will contribute to a story that is related to the course's content
- Learners will work with other learners in building a story that elaborates on course topics
- Learners will identify the basic elements that can create a story

Collaborative Learning

Small groups (5 to 7 learners)

Recommended e-Learning Experience

Learner—Novice
Facilitator—Novice

Mode

Asynchronous

Time Required

Two to three days (once-a-day minimum learner participation)

Materials

- Facilitator and learner access to an online asynchronous discussion board
- Facilitator and learner access to email

Preparation

1. Assign groups of five to nine learners each.
2. Create a forum in the course's asynchronous discussion board for each group.
3. Create a forum in the course's asynchronous discussion board for the final stories from each group.
4. Identify a goal or topic for the activity. For example, the goal for the activity may be to develop a story that (a) provides new learners with information on how to be successful in future offerings of the current course, (b) illustrates the relationship between two of the issues discussed in the course, or (c) offers a condensed version of course readings that learners could use in reviewing for an end-of-course test or professional examination.

Process

1. Email learners the instructions for the activity, as well as the names and email addresses of their group members.
2. Have each group develop a story with five basic elements.*
   - *The platform*: this provides the context for the story. For example, "Once upon a time. . . [there was a student taking an online course but struggling]."

*Based on Koppett and Richter (2001).

- *The catalyst:* this provides the reason that the story is being told. For example, "And one day. . . [the facilitator asked the student to write an essay describing her study habits]."

- *The consequences:* this provides the suspense or tension in the story. For example, "Because of that. . . [the student had to monitor her study habits for several days]."

- *The climax:* this provides the end to the tension that built up in the story. For example, "Until finally. . . [she discovered that she was not using the online tools to her advantage]."

- *The resolution:* this provides a conclusion and lessons learned from the story. For example, "Ever since then. . . [she has used instant messengers to keep in touch with her fellow students]."

3. Inform learners that individual team members can each contribute a single element (which will later be combined to form a story), or that the team can work to develop the entire story together as a group. In either case, the activity will require the group members to organize and work together in completing the story. All of the stories must, however, include all five elements.

4. Have teams post their final stories to the designated discussion board.

5. Encourage learners to review the stories developed by other groups and to discuss how the development of the story challenged and changed the team's dynamics.

Facilitator Notes

- The Telling a Story activity can also be done in a short period of time using a synchronous chat room instead of an asynchronous discussion board.

- You could also use the activity as an individual exercise in which each learner creates a story of his or her own to share with peers.

30

Evaluating Online Resources

Activity Summary

The Evaluating Online Resources activity can be used in most any online course to motivate learners to analyze and appraise online resources (or other course-related materials) in order to evaluate their quality, reliability, and utility.

Goals

- Learners will evaluate online resources for quality, reliability, and utility
- Learners will work with their peers to assess course-related resources
- Learners will build skills necessary for effective online synchronous discussions

Collaborative Learning

Small groups (3, 6, or 9 learners)

Recommended e-Learning Experience

Learner—Novice
Facilitator—Novice

Mode

Asynchronous

Time Required

Two to three days (once-a-day minimum learner participation)

Materials

- Facilitator and learner access to an online asynchronous discussion board
- Facilitator and learner access to email
- (Optional) Facilitator and learner access to a synchronous chat room

Preparation

1. Create groups of three, six, or nine learners each.
2. Identify at least an equal number of online resources related to the course content (webpages, online journal articles, online readings) as there are groups.
3. Create a forum in the course's asynchronous discussion board for each group.

Process

1. Email the learners with the instructions for the activity, the names of their group members, and the online resource(s) assigned to their group.
2. Provide each learner with evaluation criteria (that is, quality, reliability, or utility) for the activity. A sample list of evaluation criteria is provided below.*

*Guidelines are described in more detail in Watkins and Corry, 2005.

Information Quality

- Are there broad generalizations?
- Is a publication (or last updated) date provided?
- Are the facts consistent throughout the resource (as well as with other resources)?
- Are there grammatical or spelling errors?
- Is the information from an online database?
- Are there biases or assumptions apparent in the resource?
- Is there a comprehensive review of other resources on the topic?
- Does the author provide clear citations and references?
- Is the information presented original, or the author's interpretation of others' work?
- Does the resource provide additional resources (links, articles) that support the quality of the information?

Source Reliability

- Does the resource include contact information for the author?
- What are the author's credentials on the topic?
- Does the resource publisher have a credible reputation?
- Is the resource sponsored by a reliable organization?
- Was the resource peer reviewed (or better yet, blind peer reviewed)?
- Can you contact the author to verify information?

Information Utility

- Does the resource provide information related to the course topic?

- Does the resource provide information that will help you study the topic for the course?

- Is the resource written for the correct audience level related to this course (for example, is the intended audience for the resource elementary school, high school, college, or working professional learners)?

- Does the resource provide an adequate and appropriate level of detail for the course?

3. Have individual learners evaluate their assigned online resource(s) using the criteria you provided.

4. Have groups of learners discuss and come to agreement on an overall evaluation of the online resource(s).

5. Have each group post a final team evaluation of the assigned online resource(s) to their discussion forum with the subject line "Group Evaluation—Final."

Facilitator Notes

- You may also want to have learner groups identify their own online resource to be evaluated. This will typically add one to two extra days to the activity, as groups may require extra time to reach agreement on the resource to evaluate.

- As a variation you could also have learner groups identify their own additional criteria for evaluating the online resource.

31

Learner-Crafted Scavenger Hunts

Activity Summary

As a tool for encouraging greater interaction among learners in a course, you can use Learner-Crafted Scavenger Hunts to either introduce learners to a course topic or provide for more comprehensive exploration of issues that are essential to a course.

Goals

- Learners will identify essential facts from online resources
- Learners will create a scavenger hunt for their peers to explore online resources that are related to course content
- Learners will identify and locate course-related online resources
- Learners will search online resources in order to answer specific questions
- Learners will be more effective users of online resources throughout the course

Collaborative Learning

Large groups (all learners in a course)

Recommended e-Learning Experience

Learner—Novice
Facilitator—Novice

Mode
Asynchronous

Time Required
Three to five days (once-a-day minimum learner participation)

Materials
Instructor and learner access to an online asynchronous discussion board

Preparation
1. Select a course-related topic for the activity.
2. Determine an appropriate number of scavenger hunt items each learner is to create for the topic. For example, six to ten scavenger hunt items per learner would likely be appropriate for a four- to five-day activity.
3. Create sample online scavenger hunt items. For example:
   - What are three techniques commonly used to evaluate the responsiveness of customer service departments?
   - What tools are available in Microsoft Windows XP to establish a firewall for a local area network?
   - The idea of celebrating Father's Day began in 1910. How many years passed before it was made an official holiday?
   - In June of 1788, two states entered the Union. Which states were these?
4. Create a forum in the course's asynchronous discussion board.

Process

1. Email learners with instructions for creating and posting scavenger hunt items.

2. Have learners develop course-related items for their scavenger hunts.

3. Have learners post their complete scavenger hunts to the discussion forum. When a learner has posted a scavenger hunt item, no learners after that time can post the same item or an item that is considered to be too similar.

4. Encourage (or require) learners to complete a number of scavenger hunts posted by their peers.

5. End the activity by having each learner post the answers to his or her scavenger hunt.

Facilitator Notes

As a variation, have learners work in teams to develop scavenger hunt items for the activity. Teams could then compete in completing the scavenger hunts developed by other groups of learners in the course.

32

Role Reversal

Activity Summary

By using the Role Reversal format for synchronous or asynchronous course discussions, you can engage learners and offer individuals the opportunity to facilitate group discussions. During the activity you, as the facilitator, will participate in discussions as a learner. You will still have the opportunity to move the discussion in useful directions by asking questions and making comments in the role of a learner.

Goals

- Learners will play the role of the facilitator during the activity
- Learners will lead online discussions on course-related topics
- Learners will develop the necessary skills for facilitating online activities

Collaborative Learning

Medium groups (8 to 15 learners)

Recommended e-Learning Experience

Learner—Novice
Facilitator—Novice

Mode

Asynchronous or Synchronous

Time Required

Not applicable (Role Reversal is a variation to almost any other online activity)

Materials

- Facilitator and learner access to an online asynchronous discussion board
- Facilitator and learner access to online synchronous chat room
- Facilitator and learner access to email

Preparation

1. Select an activity from your online course where additional learner interactions are desired.
2. Assign learners to collaborative groups of eight to fifteen for the activity.
3. Identify one learner from each group to facilitate the activity (that is, reverse roles with you).
4. Create either an asynchronous discussion forum in the course's discussion board or synchronous chat room for each group (depending on the activity to which you are adding the Role Reversal variation).

Process

1. Email activity facilitators for each group (a) a description of the activity, (b) expectations of the facilitator during the activity, and (c) a list of learners in the collaborative group to which they have been assigned.

2. Inform all learners that their peers will facilitate the activity.

3. Give facilitators one to two days to prepare for their leading roles in the activity.

4. Have facilitators lead the synchronous or asynchronous discussions of the activity (that is, asking questions, responding to questions, posting additional information, directing the discussion, identifying the order of learners to ask questions in synchronous discussions, and providing feedback).

5. Take part in the activity from the role of a learner (that is, ask questions and make comments).

6. Have facilitators post at the end of the activity at least three lessons they learned about e-learning from the experience of reversing roles with the course facilitator.

Facilitator Notes

As a variation to the Role Reversal activity, assign pairs or teams of learners to play the role of facilitator during the activity. This variation can be useful for online activities with complex course materials.

33

Collaborative WebQuests

Activity Summary

The Collaborative WebQuest activity engages learners in the use of the World Wide Web in order to complete a task related to the course. As a collaborative learning activity, WebQuests can be used to focus groups of learners on a task while providing a variety of online resources necessary for completing their assignments.*

Goals

- Learners will utilize Web resources to complete a task
- Learners will work with their peers to complete a course-related task
- Learners will build skills for interacting with other learners in course

Collaborative Learning

Small groups (3 to 5 learners)

Recommended e-Learning Experience

Learner—Novice
Facilitator—Novice

*WebQuests are based on the research of Dr. Bernie Dodge at San Diego State University. For additional information please see <http://webquest.sdsu.edu/>.

Mode

Asynchronous

Time Required

Three to five days (once-a-day minimum learner participation)

Materials

- Facilitator and learner access to an online asynchronous discussion board
- Facilitator and learner access to the World Wide Web
- Facilitator and learner access to email

Preparation

1. Select a course-related topic that has multiple resources available on the World Wide Web (for example, sexual harassment, Mars exploration, distance education, brain research).

2. Prepare a brief introduction on the selected topic, possibly including journal articles, readings from a text, newspaper stories, other background resources, or materials that you prepare.

3. Develop a task or assignment related to the selected topic. Tasks can range from case-based questions to the development of portfolios on the selected topic. Typically you will want the task to result in a product that can be submitted by the learner groups (such as a report, presentation, portfolio, or paper). For example, a Collaborative WebQuest task could be as follows:

"To complete this WebQuest, you should work as a team to develop an annotated Webliography of online resources related to the development of leadership within sales teams. In addition to the URL, each online resource should include a two- to three-paragraph annotation (summary) describing the website's content, the leadership theory being applied, the practical application of the content to sales teams, as well as additional resources that were described in the website. Your team is responsible for submitting at least ten annotated Web resources."

4. Identify a list of additional online resources that learners should use to complete the activity.

5. Create groups of three to five learners each.

6. Create a forum in the course's asynchronous discussion board for each group.

Process

1. Email learners instructions for the activity, the names of learners in their collaborative groups, and a list of recommended steps or procedures for completing the task. For example, you could provide the following recommended procedures for completing a Collaborative WebQuest:

   • Select a team leader who will be responsible for assigning tasks and submitting the final product;

   • Identify the strengths of individual team members in relation to the WebQuest task;

   • Assign Web resources to be reviewed and summarized by team members;

   • Assign a team member to create a first draft of the assigned product;

- Determine a process for reviewing and editing the draft product; and

- Team leader submits the final product to the facilitator.

2. Have learners collaborate in completing the assigned task.

3. Monitor the discussion forums for each collaborative group.

4. Have each group's team leader email you the product of the WebQuest task when they are finished with the activity.

Facilitator Notes

As a variation to the Collaborative WebQuest, you could also utilize individual WebQuests within courses with a smaller number of learners. In addition, after completing individual WebQuests, you could introduce more interactivity to the exercise by having learners share their results with their peers and rank online resources for their usefulness in completing the task.

34

In the News

Activity Summary

The In the News activity capitalizes on the number of current event news reports available on the World Wide Web. From technological innovations to educational reform and from new management books to global economics, a large number of news stories available online can be used to engage learners in discussions on most any course topic.

Goals

- Learners will use the Web to locate news articles related to a course topic
- Learners will share online resources to expand course discussions
- Learners will build online communication skills

Collaborative Learning

Small groups (5 to 10 learners)

Recommended e-Learning Experience

Learner—Novice
Facilitator—Novice

Mode

Asynchronous

Time Required

Three to five days (once-a-day minimum learner participation)

Materials

- Facilitator and learner access to an online asynchronous discussion board
- Facilitator and learner access to the World Wide Web
- Facilitator and learner access to email

Preparation

1. Form collaborative groups of five to ten learners each.
2. Create a forum in the course's asynchronous discussion board for each group.
3. Create a forum in the course's asynchronous discussion board for group recommendations
4. Identify a course-related topic for each group.

Process

1. Email learners instructions for the activity, names of peers in the collaborative groups, and their groups' assigned topics for the activity.
2. Require each learner to identify a recent news article that is available online and that is related to the assigned topic.
3. Have each learner write a two- to three-paragraph summary of the news report he or she identified.
4. Have each learner post his or her summary and link (URL) for the news article to his or her group's discussion forum.

5. Assign each group the task of discussing each of the news articles posted by learners in their group. Each group should select one article identified within their group that they would recommend to their peers in other collaborative groups.

6. Have each group post in the designated discussion forum the learner summary of the selected news article that they would like to recommend to their peers.

7. Encourage learners to review the recommended news stories that were selected by learners in other collaborative groups.

Facilitator Notes

As an alternative to each collaborative group being assigned a different course-related topic, assign the same topic to each of the collaborative groups. This variation works very well when the online course has ten to fifteen learners in total.

35

Varied Reactions

Activity Summary

The Varied Reactions activity uses current events to engage learners in discussions and to examine multiple perspectives on topics, issues, or themes in an online course. Assigning each learner to varying roles and perspectives with regard to a range of news events encourages learners to appreciate the value of the perspectives of their peers and can assist them in developing skills for communicating effectively online.*

Goals

- Learners will reflect on current events from assigned perspectives
- Learners will react to news events from various assigned perspective throughout the course
- Learners will build skills for interacting online with their peers

Collaborative Learning

Small groups (5 to 7 learners each)

Recommended e-Learning Experience

Learner—Novice
Facilitator—Novice

*Based in part on an activity by Ko & Rossen (2004).

Mode
Asynchronous

Time Required
One hour, five to seven times during a course

Materials
- Facilitator and learner access to an online asynchronous discussion board
- Facilitator and learner access to email

Preparation
1. Form collaborative groups of five to seven learners each.
2. Create a forum in the course's asynchronous discussion board for each collaborative group.
3. Identify five to seven roles or perspectives learners can have on current news events. You should identify the same number of roles or perspectives as you have members in each collaborative group. Several examples include:
   - The believer of anything
   - The informed advocate
   - The nay-sayer
   - The disagreer
   - The supportive non-believer
   - The devil's advocate
   - The reporter who wrote the article
   - The individual at the center of the news event
   - The reader who challenges the facts in all news stories
   - The scientist who asks lots of questions

- The politician who is looking for an angle
- The middle school student who knows nothing other than what is in the article
- The teacher who wants students to learn from the article
- The Web-surfer who finds lots of related websites

Process

1. Identify a current event from a news website. Ideally, the news report or article will have some link to the current course topic, issue, or theme.

2. Email learners the link to the news article or story and their assigned role in reacting to the news event.

3. Require learners to contribute their reactions to the news event, from the perspective of their assigned roles, to their collaborative group's discussion forum. Each reaction should be one to three paragraphs long and include at the end a description of the learner's assigned perspective for the current round of the activity.

4. Identify four to six additional current event news stories related to course topics, issues, or themes during the course, each time assigning learners to a new role or perspective for their reactions to the news event.

5. Encourage learners to review the reactions of peers in their collaborative groups, noting that each peer is reacting to the news story from a perspective that may not be his or her own true response.

Facilitator Notes

You could use the Varied Reactions activity many times during a course, and offer learners the opportunity to contribute news stories that they identify.

36

Learner-Crafted Case Studies

Activity Summary

Having learners develop and share case studies can be an effective technique for engaging learners in exercises that utilize analysis skills, problem-solving techniques, peer collaboration, and/or the application of course materials in "real world" contexts. The Learner-Crafted Case Studies activity offers a structure for the collaborative development and sharing of case studies.

Goals

- Learners will collaborate with their group members in the development of a case study
- Learners will build skills for interacting online with their peers
- Learners will apply course materials to "real world" problems

Collaborative Learning

Small groups (3 to 5 learners each)

Recommended e-Learning Experience

Learner—Novice
Facilitator—Novice

Mode

Asynchronous

Time Required

Six or more days (once-a-day minimum learner participation)

Materials

- Facilitator and learner access to an online asynchronous discussion board
- Facilitator and learner access to email

Preparation

1. Form collaborative groups of three to five learners each.
2. Select a distinct course topic, issue, or theme for each collaborative group.
3. Create a forum in the course's asynchronous discussion board for each collaborative group.
4. Create a forum in the course's asynchronous discussion board for the finished case studies.

Process

1. Email learners with the names of their peers in their collaborative groups and their assigned course topics.
2. Have learners in each group work together to create a single case study focused on the application of course content to a specific "real world" problem or situation. Group case studies can be written as an exercise for individuals to complete or for teams to work on collaboratively. Case studies are generally two to three pages long, written for other learners as the primary audience, and attempt to provide just enough information for the reader to complete a task or answer a question.

Each case study should include:

- Context and background information
- Characters (for example, supervisor, employee, client)
- Time frame (for example, In 2003. . ., or Last month. . .)
- Clear description of a problem or issue to be resolved
- Necessary information for making a successful decision
- Task to be completed or question to be answered

Below is a condensed example:

"Rachel is a friend from college and she often calls you with questions regarding her work. For the past six months, Rachel has been working as an online trainer for a medium-size company that creates customized software applications for small businesses. The company is about three years old, and she reports directly to the company's founder. While Rachel has a bachelor's degree in business and five years of experience as a trainer, the founder of the company likes to maintain control over the training curriculum, schedule, and evaluations.

"Two months ago the founder of the company decided that it would be good to include a skills-based test on the company's new software product at the end of each training course. Since that time he has been pressuring Rachel to incorporate skills-based evaluation items into the training evaluations for each online course, even though she continues to insist that the current training curriculum was not designed or developed to provide the necessary skills for learners to successfully complete the skills-based evaluations.

"Last week the founder of the company stopped by Rachel's office and insisted that she include the questions in her evaluations for the current training courses. As a friend and informal mentor, what advice would you give Rachel?"

3. Have collaborative groups post their teams' case studies to the designated discussion forum.

4. Assign groups to complete the case study tasks of at least one other collaborative group from the course.

Facilitator Notes

- After using the Learner-Crafted Case Studies activity in a number of courses, you should have a robust set of case studies that can be used independently of the activity or as sample case studies for future collaborative groups.

- As a variation to the activity, select a single topic, issue, or theme from the course. Each collaborative group would then develop a unique case study around the same topic and share those at the end of the activity for their peers to review and complete.

37

Dear ADDIE Letters

Activity Summary

Online courses can use this familiar format for seeking advice to engage learners in class discussions on almost any topic. By asking learners to respond to a Dear ADDIE Letter that you develop, you can assist them in exploring a of variety topics, issues, or themes in your course.

Goals

- Learners will collaborate with their group members to compose a response to the assigned Dear ADDIE Letter
- Learners will build skills for interacting online with their peers
- Learners will review course materials in responding to the assigned Dear ADDIE letter

Collaborative Learning

Small groups (3 to 5 learners each)

Recommended e-Learning Experience

Learner—Novice
Facilitator—Novice

Mode

Asynchronous

Time Required

Two to three days

Materials

- Facilitator and learner access to an online asynchronous discussion board
- Facilitator and learner access to email

Preparation

1. Form collaborative groups of three to five learners each.
2. Create a forum in the course's asynchronous discussion board for each collaborative group.
3. Create a forum in the course's asynchronous discussion board for collaborative groups to post their responses to the Dear ADDIE letter.
4. Develop a Dear ADDIE letter that seeks advice from collaborative groups with regard to a "real world" situation that requires the application of course content to resolve.

Dear ADDIE letters should include the following elements:

- Introduction
- Background and context
- Problem to be solved or decision to be made
- Request for advice

For example:

"Dear ADDIE,

> "I am writing for advice on how to implement performance-improvement measures at my company. A few weeks ago I became an overwhelmed new hire at a corporate training vendor.

> "My new employer is a small company that develops and delivers customized technology training to corporate customers. We also deliver a variety of standard computer-skills training classes (Windows, Word, Excel, HTML, Flash, etc.) from our extensive catalog. All of the training is classroom based and I lead the training design and development team. . .

> ". . .There are a growing number of customer complaints about staff turnover. A project starts with one rep and closes with another who is not adequately informed. Clients no longer feel secure when a different representative approaches them each time without knowing the background of the firm's relationship. . .

> ". . . What should I do?

"Sincerely,

"Dazed in Dallas"

Process

1. Post the Dear ADDIE letter that you have developed to each of the collaborative groups.

2. Have the learners in each group work together in developing a response to the letter, using a variety of class texts, articles, websites, and other resources in providing useful advice to resolve the problem(s) described in the letter.

3. Require each collaborative group to post a response to the designated discussion forum.

4. Encourage learners to review the response letters from the other collaborative groups.

Facilitator Notes

Dear ADDIE Letters can also be assigned to individual learners or to all of the learners in the class as an alternative to the small group format suggested above.

38

Electronic Portfolios

Activity Summary

Electronic Portfolios can be a useful strategy for assessing learners in an online course. By having learners provide a diverse selection of reports, presentations, Web resources, draft documents, and other files, you can effectively assess their performance in online courses on most any topic.

Goals

- Learners will develop a diverse portfolio of products illustrating their performance in the course
- Learners will review course materials in organizing their electronic portfolios

Collaborative Learning

Large group (all learners in a course)

Recommended e-Learning Experience

Learner—Novice
Facilitator—Novice

Mode

Asynchronous

Time Required

Two to three days

Materials

- Facilitator and learner access to an online asynchronous discussion board
- Facilitator and learner access to file compression software (for example, the free software WinZip)
- Facilitator and learner access to email

Preparation

1. Identify multiple activities and assignments from your course that learners can submit as a portfolio of their performance in the course. These can include reports, presentations, papers, essays, peer feedback, Web resources, Webliographies, and other products developed for the course (in addition, learners should include draft files of reports, papers, and essays that were developed in the course and any feedback you provided on the drafts).
2. Create a forum in the course's asynchronous discussion board for the activity.

Process

1. Email learners at the beginning of the course with directions for saving and organizing files for the Electronic Portfolio. Include with the email a list of all the activities and assignments that are expected to be in each learner's portfolio.
2. Have learners develop the activities and assignments throughout the course as independent files, saving the draft files that illustrate their development process and your feedback.

3. Require learners to write cover letters for their Electronic Portfolios, containing a list of the files included in the portfolio and a discussion of how the individual elements illustrate their performance in the course.

4. Have learners use file compression software (for example, WinZip) to combine/compress the multiple files required for the Electronic Portfolio, including the cover letter, into a single file.

5. Have learners attach their Electronic Portfolio files to a posting in the discussion forum.

6. Encourage learners to review the Electronic Portfolios of their peers.

7. Provide learners with feedback on the reports, projects, papers, or other elements included in the portfolios.

Facilitator Notes

- Learners with advanced technical skills can also be encouraged to build their Electronic Portfolios as a website with links to each of the portfolio files.

- Novice e-learners may require instructions for using recommended compression software. These directions are typically available on the download website for the software and don't require advanced technical skills.

39

My Reactions

Activity Summary

The My Reactions activity can help learners organize and share their reactions, perspectives, opinions, and evaluations of readings they complete for an online course. As a collaborative exercise, this activity provides learners with the opportunity to summarize their reactions to a course reading around three concepts: what they agree with in the reading, what they disagree with, and what they find to be interesting.*

Goals

- Learners will complete course readings
- Learners will identify in readings what they agree with, disagree with, and find interesting
- Learners will share their reactions to the course readings with their peers

Collaborative Learning

Large groups (all learners in a course)

Recommended e-Learning Experience

Learner—Novice
Facilitator—Novice

*Based in part on DeBono (1994).

Mode
Asynchronous

Time Required
Two to three days

Materials

- Facilitator and learner access to an online asynchronous discussion board
- Facilitator and learner access to email

Preparation

1. Identify one or more readings that are required for the course (articles, chapters from a book, reports, websites, etc.).
2. Create a forum in the course's asynchronous discussion forum for each reading selected for the activity.

Process

1. Inform learners of the required readings for the activity.
2. Require each learner to identify at least one element of each course reading that he or she agrees with, at least one element he or she disagrees with, and at least one element he or she finds to be interesting.
3. Have each learner write one to three paragraphs (per reading) describing his or her reactions to the required reading (including a description of what was agreed with, disagreed with, and found interesting).

4. Require each learner to post his or her reaction in the designated discussion forum for each course reading.

5. Encourages learners to review the posted reactions of their peers.

Facilitator Notes

As a variation, have learners work in small groups of three to five to compare and discuss their reactions prior to posting them to the discussion forum.

40

Annotated Webliographies

Activity Summary

Annotated Webliographies is a collaborative activity that encourages learners to identify, summarize, and share World Wide Web resources on course-related topics. This activity can be used in almost any online course to engage and focus learners in their exploration of the Web, as well as to organize the sharing of Web resources among peers.

Goals

- Learners will identify useful Web resources related to course topics
- Learners will write an annotation describing the Web resources they identify
- Learners will share the Web resources they identify with their peers

Collaborative Learning

Medium groups (8 to 15 learners)

Recommended e-Learning Experience

Learner—Novice
Facilitator—Novice

Mode

Asynchronous

Time Required
Three to five days

Materials
- Facilitator and learner access to an online asynchronous discussion board
- Facilitator and learner access to email

Preparation
1. Identify a course topic, issue, or theme for the Annotated Webliographies activity.
2. Form collaborative groups of eight to fifteen learners each.
3. Create a forum in the course's asynchronous discussion board for each collaborative group.

Process
1. Require each learner to identify five to ten websites related to the assigned course topic, issue, or theme.
2. Have learners compose a 200- to 250-word annotation for each website they identify. The annotation must include at least the following elements (you may want to require additional elements, depending on the focus of the course):
   - The URL;
   - The date the website was accessed;
   - Who owns and/or maintains the website;
   - A description of what is contained on the website; and
   - A discussion of how the website is useful in relation to the course.

3. Have learners collect their five to ten entries into one document.

4. Have learners aggregate their Annotated Webliographies in one posting to their collaborative group's discussion forum. When a learner has posted a website in his or her annotated Webliography, no other learners in the collaborative group can post an annotation of that same website later.

5. Require learners to review and discuss the annotated Webliographies within the collaborative group, identifying common themes among websites, sharing useful online resources, and noting how the websites will be useful during the course.

Facilitator Notes

- As a variation, assign each collaborative group to a different course topic, issue, or theme for their Annotated Webliographies.

- The Annotated Webliographies activity can also be done as an individual activity with all learners in the course sharing their Webliographies in a single discussion forum. For large courses it is, however, unlikely that learners will be able to review the Web resources identified by all other learners in the course.

Revise, Revise, Revise

Activity Summary

The development of quality papers or essays in almost any course (online or in the classroom) typically requires feedback and guidance from the facilitator on several preliminary drafts. The Revise, Revise, Revise activity can guide learners through several strategies for developing effective written communication skills by focusing on three revision cycles; limiting, adding, and clarifying.*

Goals

- Learners will develop quality papers or essays
- Learners will complete revision cycles in developing their papers or essays
- Learners will reflect on the writing process and effective written communication skills

Collaborative Learning

Individual (all learners in a course)

Recommended e-Learning Experience

Learner—Novice
Facilitator—Novice

*Based in part on ideas from a workshop with Toby Fulwiler (2004).

Mode

Asynchronous

Time Required

Six or more days (typically two to three weeks)

Materials

Facilitator and learner access to email.

Preparation

Identify a paper or essay assignment that is appropriate for the course.

Process

1. Email learners informing them of the paper or essay assignment and the drafts that will be required (but not graded) prior to submission of the final paper.
2. Have each learner complete a rough draft of the assignment.
3. Review and provide feedback to learners on draft assignments.
4. Require each learner to review the feedback provided on his or her rough draft and complete a revision for the second draft (for example, a revision being 75 percent or more new material, not just edits).

   For the first revision learners should focus on limiting their papers or essays. To do this, learners could:

   • Limit time, place, or action in the paper or essay
   • Limit the scope of the paper or essay
   • Limit the focus of the paper or essay

For example, if the initial draft of the essay focused on the application of technology skills in working with the disabled, the learner may choose to limit the scope of the paper or essay to the application of computer keyboarding skills to working with the blind.

4. Have each learner submit a copy of the second (limited) draft of the assignment by an assigned date.

5. Provide guidance and/or feedback to learners (but do not grade draft assignments).

6. Require each learner to review his or her second draft and complete a revision for the third draft (for example, a revision being 50 percent or more new material, not just edits). For the next revision, learners should focus on adding an element to their paper or essay. In adding an element, learners could:

   • Add dialogue or descriptions

   • Add an interview or observations

   • Add secondary sources of information

   For example, if the second draft of a paper focused on the development of modern theories in the treatment of depression, the learner may choose to add information gained through interviews with three or four leading psychologists.

7. Have each learner submit a copy of the third (added element) draft of the assignment by an assigned date.

8. Provide guidance and/or feedback to learners (but do not grade draft assignments).

9. Require each learner to review the third draft and complete a final revision of the paper or essay. In developing the final version, learners should focus on editing the paper or essay. In editing their paper or essay, learners could:

- Take out unnecessary information
- Ensure the agreement of verb tenses
- Check for grammatical errors
- Check spelling
- Have a peer review the final version

10. Have each learner submit a final copy of the assignment by an assigned date.

11. Review the draft assignments prior to grading the final papers or essays.

Facilitator Notes

As a variation, limit the number of drafts submitted by learners to just one (just a draft that is limited or a draft that has added elements), or expand the activity to include additional drafts, each with a different theme for improving the paper or essay (for example, a draft in which the learner switches perspective or position, a draft in which the learner transforms the paper into a news article, letter to the editor, or book review).

42

Class Book

Activity Summary

The Class Book activity produces a valuable resource that learners can use long after the online course has ended. A collection of the reports, papers, essays, or presentations submitted by learners during a course, the Class Book becomes a resource that learners can use to review course material, troubleshoot problems on the job, or share with colleagues.

Goals

- Learners will submit reports, papers, essays, or presentations for the Class Book
- Learners will collaborate with their peers in selecting content for the Class Book

Collaborative Learning

Large groups (all learners in a course)

Recommended e-Learning Experience

Learner—Novice
Facilitator—Novice

Mode

Asynchronous

Time Required

Three to five days (once-a-day minimum learner participation)

Materials

- Facilitator and learner access to an online asynchronous discussion board

- Facilitator and learner access to email

Preparation

Create a forum in the course's asynchronous discussion board for the activity.

Process

1. Have learners post to the discussion forum which reports, papers, essays, or presentations they would like to have represented in a Class Book that will be available to them after the course has ended as a tool for applying the course material to their work. These can be completed assignments or activities from the course or materials that they have developed outside of the course that could be of value to other learners when they apply course concepts in their work. Examples could include notes from study groups, diagrams of complex course concepts, or presentations learners have given on course-related materials at professional conferences.

2. Develop a table of contents for the Class Book based on the desired elements posted by learners.

3. Request that learners submit reports, papers, essays, or presentations that they have created for the course and that fit with desired contents of the Class Book. Inform learners that any files submitted to be included in the Class Book are not confidential.

4. Collect and organize the files submitted by learners.

5. Cut and paste all of the reports, papers, and essays into one word processing file, and likewise combine all of the presentations into one presentation file.

6. Post a copy of all the submitted works to the discussion forum.

7. Have learners vote on which files they would find most useful in a Class Book.

8. Tally the votes and delete the reports, papers, essay, or presentations that received the least votes from the learners.

9 Post the revised file(s) to the discussion forum as the Class Book.

10. Encourage learners to review the book's contents and to save a copy to their personal computer for later use after the online course has ended.

Facilitator Notes

- As a variation, request that one or more learners work as a collaborative group to identify, collect, organize, and combine the files for the Class Book instead of doing this yourself.

- For learners or facilitators with advanced technology skills, you could also create a Class Book website where each element of the book is linked from a primary Class Book webpage.

43

Discussion Summaries

Activity Summary

Discussion Summaries are a useful technique for engaging learners in the processes of reviewing and reflecting on course discussions. Learners providing the discussion summary for assigned forums can build the skills related to analyzing and synthesizing information, while aiding their peers by providing useful resources for reviewing course materials.

Goals

- Learners will review and reflect on course discussions
- Learners will analyze and synthesize course discussions in writing a summary
- Learners will study course content by reviewing discussion summaries posted by their peers

Collaborative Learning

Large group (all learners in a course)

Recommended e-Learning Experience

Learner—Novice
Facilitator—Novice

Mode

Asynchronous

Time Required

30 to 60 minutes (one time per learner)

Materials

Facilitator and learner access to an online asynchronous discussion board

Preparation

1. Create a forum in the course's asynchronous discussion board for the discussion summaries.

2. Assign each learner in the course to one or more asynchronous discussions planned for the course. You will want at least one summary per course discussion.

Process

1. Have learners review and reflect on all of the postings included in their assigned asynchronous discussion (ideally, the day after the discussion has ended).

2. Have each learner compose a two- to three-paragraph summary of the discussion. In the summary learners should include major points made during the conversation, critical elements from course materials, Web resources described by participants, as well as other essential information gleaned from the asynchronous discussion.

3. Require each learner to post his or her summary of the course discussion to the designated discussion forum.

4. Encourage learners to review the discussion summaries posted by their peers.

Facilitator Notes

You may want to copy and paste each of the discussion summaries from a course into a single word processing document that can be emailed to learners as a tool for reviewing course materials.

Critical Incidents

Activity Summary

The Critical Incidents activity engages online learners by illustrating the application of course content to the "real life" problems and opportunities of their peers.

Goals

- Learners will identify the application of course concepts or proficiencies that they have applied in their "real life" outside of the classroom
- Learners will share their experiences in applying course content with their peers
- Learners will reflect on the experiences of their peers

Collaborative Learning

Large groups (all learners in a course)

Recommended e-Learning Experience

Learner—Novice
Facilitator—Novice

Mode

Asynchronous

Time Required

Two to three days (once-a-day minimum learner participation)

Materials

Facilitator and learner access to an online asynchronous discussion board

Preparation

1. Identify three to five critical concepts or proficiencies from your online course.

2. Compose a critical incident question for each concept or proficiency you identified. For example:

   - "Can you describe an experience in the past when you have applied the Pythagorean Theorem in solving a problem on the job?"

   - "Describe a time when you used your training in technology to resolve an issue that your division was having with its accounting practices."

   - "Describe an event during which you were to apply change-management techniques in leading a team or work group."

3. Create a forum in the course's asynchronous discussion board for each critical incident question.

Process

1. Have learners in the course review each of the critical incident questions.

2. Require each learner in the course to respond to at least one of the critical incident questions. Each posted response should be at least three to five paragraphs long and contain:

- Context and background information;
- Characters (for example, supervisor, employee, client);
- Time frame (for example, In 2003. . ., or Last month. . .); and
- Clear descriptions of the application of the course concepts or proficiencies in the Critical Incidents.

3. Encourage learners to review the posted critical incident responses of their peers.

Facilitator Notes

As a variation have the learners select the critical incident questions for use in the activity.

45

Class Memoir*

Activity Summary

Developing a class memoir can be an effective activity both for encouraging learners to reflect on their learning experiences and for developing community within an online course. As an activity that continues throughout a course, the Class Memoir activity gives all learners the opportunity to participate in creating a record (or journal) of the course experience.

Goals

- Learners will reflect on their learning experiences
- Learners will create a record (or journal) of the online course experience
- Learners will build skills for interacting online with their peers

Collaborative Learning

Large groups (all learners in a course)

Recommended e-Learning Experience

Learner—Novice
Facilitator—Novice

*Developed in collaboration with Steve Sugar.

Mode

Asynchronous

Time Required

Ongoing task throughout the course

Materials

Facilitator and learner access to an online asynchronous discussion board

Preparation

Create two forums in the course's asynchronous discussion board for the activity: one for the Class Memoir and one for participants' reflections at the end of the course after reviewing the memoir.

Process

1. Encourage learners to contribute to the first forum, the Class Memoir, throughout the course. The memoir contributions should include descriptions of course activities, assignments, discussions, readings, and other events. Unlike a group blog (see activity 60, Group Blogs) the Class Memoir is an historical document that records the learners' experiences. Contributions can include:

   - Summaries of learning experiences (activities, assignments)
   - Journal or log entries
   - Weekly reviews
   - Reflections on course discussions
   - Current events that have impacted course learners

2. Have learners review the Class Memoirs in the discussion forum at the end of the course.

3. Require learners to post two- to three-paragraph reflections in the second forum after reviewing the Class Memoir. In their reflections learners should include descriptions of how their perspectives on course topics were changed through the course experiences.

Facilitator Notes

As an alternative, create asynchronous discussion forums for each learner in the course and have individual learners keep a course journal (a journal being somewhere between a diary and course log book).

46

100 Words or Less

Activity Summary

The 100 Words or Less activity offers online learners the opportunity to interpret and share their understanding of the course topics, issues, or themes in their reading through short statements that are available to their peers in the course. As a technique that encourages learners to reflect, summarize, and share their understanding of course readings, this activity can also aid learners in developing useful e-learning study habits.

Goals

- Learners will reflect on course readings
- Learners will write down their interpretation and understanding of course topics, issues, and themes in 100 words or less
- Learners will share their interpretation of course readings with their peers
- Learners will review and reflect on the interpretations of other learners in the course

Collaborative Learning

Large groups (all learners in a course)

Recommended e-Learning Experience

Learner—Novice
Facilitator—Novice

Mode
Asynchronous

Time Required
30 to 40 minutes per learner, multiple times throughout the course

Materials
- Facilitator and learner access to an online asynchronous discussion board
- Facilitator and learner access to email

Preparation
Create a forum in the course's asynchronous discussion board for the activity.

Process
1. Email learners at the beginning of the course informing them of the 100 Words or Less discussion forum that will be available throughout the course.
2. Encourage learners to reflect on the topics, issues, and themes from their readings in the course.
3. Encourage learners to write brief (100 words or less) summaries of the interpretation and understanding of the course readings.
4. Have learners post a minimum number of summaries, for example, four or five during the course, in the activity forum to be reviewed by both you and other learners.

5. Respond to the brief summaries in the discussion forum, identifying inaccurate interpretations, offering examples, and expanding on summaries that are useful for learners as tools for reviewing course materials.

6. Encourage learners to review and comment on the postings of their peers.

Facilitator Notes

- Having learners post longer notes on course readings can also be useful. This variation on the activity encourages learners to take notes as they read course materials and also gives them the opportunity to share their understandings of course materials with their peers for further reflection and conversation.

- As an alternative, assign individual learners to create 100 Words or Less summaries of assigned readings through the course. For example, Learner A could be assigned to write a 100 Words or Less summary of Chapter 1, Section 3. After Learner A's summary is posted, other learners in the course could respond with their summaries or discussion of the assigned summary.

Section Six
Increasing Interactivity

···

WHILE INTERACTIONS WITH OTHER LEARNERS are not absolutely necessary for learning to be achieved in online courses, active participation with others is often important for engaging learners, encouraging critical thinking, challenging assumptions, developing curiosity, creating online relationships, and achieving many of the goals that may or may not be listed as the course's learning objectives. In addition, e-learning activities can many times improve the efficiency of e-learning lessons by reducing the amount of time required for achieving mastery, reducing the learners' dependence on the instructor, and utilizing the knowledge and experience of e-learners as a resource for the accomplishment of course goals.

The e-learning activities included in the following section are specifically developed to encourage additional interactions among e-learners. These activities can be used effectively at the beginning of the course to establish an engaging learning environment for participants or at later times in a course to revitalize learners who may be struggling with the isolation that can emerge in any course that is not designed to benefit from the active participation of learners. Many of the activities in this section require little time to facilitate, and several are based on games commonly used in the traditional classroom. I encourage you to review these activities both before your online course begins as well as at times during the course when you want to re-energize your online classroom.

47

Digital Chain Letter

Activity Summary

Before an online course begins or during a course, it can be motivating and useful to communicate with the learners through a digital chain letter. The Digital Chain Letter activity can provide useful introductions, establish expectations, and offer learners the opportunity to interact with their peers.

Goals

- Learners will receive an introduction to the course and the facilitator
- Learners will use email to communicate with other learners
- Learners will be more effective users of online resources throughout the course

Collaborative Learning

Small groups (4 to 7 learners)

Recommended e-Learning Experience

Learner—Novice
Facilitator—Novice

Mode

Asynchronous

Time Required

Four to seven days (approximately one day per learner)

Materials

Facilitator and learner access to email

Preparation

1. Divide learners into groups of four to seven learners each.

2. Write the initial email that will begin the Digital Chain Letter activity. The initial email should include at least the following elements:

   - Introduction to yourself and the course (one or two paragraphs)

   - Description of the activity and what next steps the learner should take

   - Instructions for forwarding the chain letter to their assigned peers

   - Instructions for including previous messages in the forwarded message

   - Ordered list of the learners in each group (including their email addresses)

   Below is a condensed example of an initial email:

   "Hello and welcome to your first training course on Improving Call Center Responsiveness. This will be the first of three online training courses that you will be taking as a new employee with our company. My name is Samuel and I will be your instructor for the next five weeks.

"To begin the course and get to know one another, we will be 'passing around' a digital chain letter. When you receive this chain letter, you should review the introductions posted by your peers, and then forward it along to the next member of the class. A list of who you should send the message to next appears at the bottom of this letter. Using the company's email system, you will use the 'forward' button to send the message to the next person on the list; this will automatically include all of the previous email introductions at the bottom of your message. When the digital chain letter makes it way back to me, I will send everyone in the course a copy to complete the chain.

"Before sending the chain letter to the next learner, you should add a two- to three-paragraph introduction. This introduction should include your name, position, when you were hired, what you hope to gain from this training course, and how you would like to use the skills from the course in your job when we are done. After adding this introduction, you can forward the chain letter to the next learner.

"I am looking forward to getting to know each of you over the next five weeks.

"Sincerely,

"Samuel

"Samuel to Ron (ron@ourcompany.com)

Ron to Terrence (terrence@ourcompany.com)

Terrence to Samantha (samantha@ourcomapny.com)

Samantha to Greg (greg@ourcompany.com)

Greg to Samuel (samuel@ourcompany.com)"

Process

1. Email the Digital Chain Letter to the first learner in each group.

2. Review the chain letter when it returns to you.

2. Send copies of each group's completed Digital Chain Letter to all learners in the course.

Facilitator Notes

*   At the mid-point of the activity email a learner in each group to determine whether the chain letter is moving from learner to learner as desired.

*   As a variation, post the completed Digital Chain Letters to an online asynchronous discussion board for all learners to review.

48

Regional Chats

Activity Summary

Online courses will often include learners from a variety of locations around the world. The Regional Chats activity can be used to facilitate synchronous group discussions with consideration to significant time-zone differences.

Goals

- Learners will participate in synchronous discussions with their peers who are located in a similar region of the world
- Learners will report on their discussions within their regional group to learners in the course who are located in various other regions
- Learners will build skills necessary for effective online synchronous discussions

Collaborative Learning

Small groups (3 to 5 learners within similar time zones)

Recommended e-Learning Experience

Learner—Moderate
Facilitator—Moderate

Mode

Synchronous and Asynchronous

Time Required

Two to three days (learner participation in at least two synchronous chats)

Materials

- Facilitator and learner access to an online asynchronous discussion board
- Facilitator and learner access to a synchronous chat room
- Facilitator and learner access to email

Preparation

1. Identify the location (country, state, and/or time zone) for each of the learners in the online course.
2. Create groups of three to five learners based around the regions (time zones).
3. Select a course-related topic for learners to discuss for twenty to thirty minutes in a synchronous chat room and then report back to their peers.
4. Establish a forum in the course's asynchronous discussion board.

Process

1. Email learners the instructions for the activity, as well as the names and email addresses of group members. In addition you may want to include a timeline for the activity, information on what the group is to discuss in their synchronous chats, suggestions for setting a time for their synchronous discussions, and what they are to report back to the other regional groups in the course in the asynchronous discussion board forum.

2. Have regional groups meet in the course's synchronous chat room to discuss the activity topic. During the chat a learner in the group should take notes and later summarize the discussions of the group.

3. Require each regional group to post a summary of the synchronous discussion to the online asynchronous discussion board.

4. Encourage learners to review the summaries posted by other regional groups.

Facilitator Notes

If your online course does not have access to synchronous chat tools within the course management system, learners can be encouraged to set up individual instant messaging accounts (for example, MSN Messenger, ICQ, AOL Messenger) to facilitate the synchronous discussion elements of this activity. If individual learners already use distinct instant messaging programs, cross-platform messenger software (for example, Trillian) can be used, for example, so MSN Messenger users can chat with ICQ users without having to create new accounts.

49

Structured Controversies

Activity Summary

The Structured Controversies activity gives learners in an online course the opportunity to debate alternative positions on topics related to the course's content. By debating alternative positions, learners can be challenged to examine the multiple perspectives on an issue and gain an appreciation for the viewpoints of others.

Goals

- Learners will participate in asynchronous debate on issues related to the course's content
- Learners will make a case for positions that may challenge their presumptions prior to the Structured Controversies activity
- Learners will develop positive online relationships with their peers
- Learners will practice their skills of effectively communicating in an asynchronous online discussion

Collaborative Learning

Small groups (teams of 2 to 4 learners)

Recommended e-Learning Experience

Learner—Novice
Facilitator—Moderate

Mode

Asynchronous

Time Required

Six days (once-a-day minimum learner participation)

Materials

- Facilitator and learner access to an online asynchronous discussion board

- Facilitator and learner access to email

- (Optional) Learner access to instant messengers or synchronous chat rooms

Preparation

1. Select an issue that has two distinct perspectives that can be contested by the learners. The issue to be debated is best stated as a statement that can be supported (by the pro or affirmative team) and refuted (by the con or negative) team.

   For example, (a) the use of calculators should be permitted during standardized tests and/or profession certification exams, (b) the growth of vegetables that come from genetically engineered seeds should be permitted, or (c) the government should provide health insurance for all citizens who are not covered through an agreement with their employers.

2. Create teams of two to four learners each.

3. Assign teams to a position on the issue (that is, pro or con, affirmative or negative).

4. Match teams for the debates (that is, pro teams versus con teams).

5. Create a forum in the course's asynchronous discussion board for each pair of teams.

Process

1. Email learners with instructions for the activity, including a list of members for each team. The following is a set of instructions you can use. You'll need to add the list of team member names.

2. On day one, monitor the pro team's position statement to ensure that it does not exceed 1,000 words since this is a replacement for the traditional time limits given a debate.

3. On day two, monitor the con team's position statement to ensure that it does not exceed 1,000 words.

4. On day three, monitor the pro team's position statement to ensure that it does not exceed 500 words.

5. On day four, monitor the con team's position statement to ensure that it does not exceed 500 words.

6. On day five, monitor the pro team's position statement to ensure that it does not exceed 500 words.

7. On day six, monitor the con team's position statement to ensure that it does not exceed 500 words.

8. After both teams have posted closing arguments, you should select a winner for the debate.

Facilitator Notes

As an alternative to having multiple debates happening simultaneously during an online course, you may choose to have a limited number of learners participate in the Structured Controversies activity while the remaining learners in the course act as the judges in determining which team won the debate. If you plan to have multiple debates throughout a course, thus allowing all learners to participate in at least one Structured Controversy activity, then this can be a useful variation and reduce the amount of organization you have to do as a facilitator.

Day One

The pro (or affirmative) team members will work together to develop statements of up to 1,000 words that support their positions on the issue you have identified for the activity. The pro team will post its statement as a single reply to the discussion forum. In the position paper the team should include at least a few of the following elements:

- Define the issue
- Endorse that the status quo isn't going to resolve the issue
- Offer a specific proposal as to what should be done
- Defend their plan to solve the issue
- Use data and references to support their statements

Day Two

The con (or negative) team members will work together to develop three to five questions for the pro (or affirmative) team as well as a statement supporting their position on the issue. The con team will post its statement as a single reply to the discussion forum. The total posting by the team (including the questions and the statement) can be no more than 1,000 words. In their statement the con team should include at least a few of the following elements:

- Question the data or references used by the pro team
- Question the logic of the plan proposed by the pro team
- Refute the parameters established by the pro team to define the issue
- Challenge the specifics of the pro team's statements and plan
- Offer an alternative proposal as to what should be done
- Defend their alternative plan to solve the issue
- Use data and references to support their statements

Day Three

The pro team is to post a single response in the discussion forum to the con team's questions and position statement posted on the second day. All of the questions posted by the con team must be addressed by the pro team. In addition, the pro team can add three to five questions challenging the statement of the con team and/or offer another statement supporting their position on the issue. A single posting of no more than 500 words should be developed by the pro team.

Day Four

The con team is to post a single response in the discussion forum to the pro team's questions and additional position statements posted on the third day. All of the questions posted by the pro team must be addressed by the con team. In addition, the con team can add three to five questions challenging the statements of the pro team and/or offering another statement supporting their position on the issue. A single posting of no more than 500 words should be developed by the con team.

Day Five

The pro team should develop a closing argument supporting its position of no more than 500 words. The statement should be posted as a single reply to the discussion forum.

Day Six

The con team should develop a closing argument supporting its position of no more than 500 words. The statement should be posted as a single reply to the discussion forum.

50

Meet an Expert

Activity Summary

The Meet an Expert activity offers online learners the familiar experiences of having a guest speaker without requiring anybody to leave the comfort of his or her home or office. In addition, by offering a structure, the activity can help ensure that the online discussion is interesting and useful for both the guest and the learners.

Goals

- Learners will have the opportunity to interact with a guest speaker
- Learners will build skills necessary for professional and effective online synchronous communications
- Learners will summarize the major topics discussed with the guest speaker

Collaborative Learning

Large groups (all learners in a course)

Recommended e-Learning Experience

Learner—Moderate
Facilitator—Moderate
Guest speaker—Moderate

Mode

Synchronous

Time Required

90 to 120 minutes (each learner having an opportunity to ask a question)

Materials

- Facilitator, guest, and learner access to an online asynchronous discussion board

- Facilitator, guest, and learner access to email

- Facilitator, guest, and learner access to a synchronous chat room

Preparation

1. Provide the learners in the course, and the invited expert, with guidelines for etiquette and participation. The guidelines should include the following, although you may want to add or subtract from this list depending on your preferences as the facilitator:

- Review the required readings and other information on the guest speaker prior to the Meet an Expert activity;

- Prepare at least one question for the guest speaker before the Meet an Expert activity begins;

- Visit the synchronous chat area of the course the day before the Meet an Expert activity to ensure that you have the necessary software applications to fully participate in the discussion (for example, new versions of Web browser software, plug-ins);

- Create a good study environment for the activity (that is, turn off email, instant messengers, television, and other distracters);
- Arrive to the Meet an Expert activity at least five minutes early;
- Do not greet the other participants when you arrive or when they arrive;
- Address your questions or comments to the guest speaker (for example, "Dr. Phillips, can you explain that concept again?");
- When possible, cut and paste the questions that you prepared prior to the Meet an Expert activity into the synchronous chat instead of typing them in at the time;
- "Raise your hand" to gain the attention of the guest speaker by posting a blank message;
- Avoid sarcasm, idioms, slang, jargon, and other statements that may lead to miscommunication;
- Leave misspelled words unless the error changes the meaning of the message.

2. Create a forum within the course's asynchronous discussion board.

3. Identify a synchronous chat room for the activity. Most online course delivery tools (for example, Blackboard®, WebCT®, LearningSpace®) offer multiple chat rooms that can be used simultaneously for group activities or alone for whole-class activities. From the available chat rooms, select a specific chat room (that is, chat room one or chat room A) for the activity.

4. Have a practice chat two days before the Meet the Expert activity for learners to verify that they have access.

5. Write a short introduction to the guest expert in your word processing program.

Process

1. Welcome the expert to the synchronous chat and cut and paste a short introduction from the word processing program into the synchronous chat room.

2. Give each learner the opportunity to ask at least one question of the guest speaker. Have the learners ask their prepared questions in alphabetical (or reverse-alphabetical) order.

3. Keep an eye on the time and let the learners and guest speaker know when there are ten minutes left in the Meet an Expert activity.

4. End the synchronous chat on time, and thank everyone for their participation.

5. Have each learner post to the asynchronous discussion forum at least three points of interest from the chat with the guest speaker.

6. Post a copy of the transcripts from the synchronous chat, if available, to the asynchronous forum.

Facilitator Notes

The Meet an Expert activity can also be done using an asynchronous discussion board, although this does require the guest speaker to participate in the discussion several times over a period of time. To facilitate an asynchronous version of the Meet an Expert activity, establish a forum in the course's asynchronous discussion board to host the activity, and then either ask the guest speaker to post an introductory set of comments for learners to respond to or ask learners to pose an initial set of questions for the guest speaker.

51

Online Study Groups

Activity Summary

Online Study Groups can provide learners with active and supportive e-learning communities. The online relationships that develop in study groups often encourage learners to share notes, ask review questions of each other, provide peer feedback, give technical support, and offer motivational support to one another.

Goals

- Learners will participate in learning communities with their peers
- Learners will use asynchronous discussion boards to build online relationship that are positive and supportive
- Learners will build skills necessary for effective online asynchronous discussions

Collaborative Learning

Large groups (all learners in a course)

Recommended e-Learning Experience

Learner—Novice
Facilitator—Novice

Mode

Asynchronous or Synchronous

Time Required

Ongoing task throughout the course

Materials

- Facilitator and learner access to an online asynchronous discussion board
- Facilitator and learner access to a synchronous chat room

Preparation

1. Organize a structure to facilitate the use of online study groups in your course. Here are some ideas for structuring online study groups within any course:

Asynchronous Study Groups
- Study groups based on major or professional roles (for example, engineers, teachers, lawyers, artists)
- Study groups assigned by last names (A through G, H through P, Q through Z)
- The "once-a-day" study group
- The "every-other-day" study group
- Study groups based on questions (such as general questions, course specifics, lesson one)
- Study groups based on assessments (for example, preparing for exam one, preparing for lesson five quiz, preparing for professional certification exam)
- Study groups based on time zones

Synchronous Study Groups
- Study groups based on time zones
- The "morning chatters" study group
- The "late night" study group

- Study groups that quiz one another (for example, Jeopardy®, Quick Recall®)
- Study groups for the "night before" the exam
- Study groups assigned by last names (A through G, H through P, Q through Z)

2. Either assign learners to study groups or let learners join groups as the course progresses. Both techniques can be engaging and create an online community.

3. Create the necessary forums in the course's asynchronous discussion board and/or synchronous chat rooms for the study groups.

Process

1. Inform learners that these resources are available for online study groups.

2. If applicable, inform learners of their assigned online study group.

3. Monitor learner participation in online study groups. For example, when a learner struggles with a course activity or assignment, you may want to send him or her an email reminder of the value in participating in online study groups.

Facilitator Notes

There are numerous variations you can use for establishing Online Study Groups within your course. In addition to the asynchronous discussion board and synchronous chat room study groups described in this activity, you may also want to consider using email study groups. Typically these Online Study Groups can be useful for creating community and enhancing the online experience of learners through interactions with their peers.

52

Town Hall Meeting

Activity Summary

The Town Hall Meeting format can be extremely useful for communicating with a large number of online learners in structured synchronous discussion. By offering learners an organized forum for asking questions on course-related topics, this activity can remove the confusion that often accompanies unstructured synchronous discussions.

Goals

- Learners will participate in synchronous discussions with their peers
- Learners will have the opportunity to ask questions and discuss issues as a group
- Learners will build skills necessary for effective online synchronous discussions

Collaborative Learning

Large groups (all learners in a course)

Recommended e-Learning Experience

Learner—Moderate
Facilitator—Moderate

Mode

Synchronous

Time Required

75 to 90 minutes

Materials

- Facilitator and learner access to a synchronous chat room
- Facilitator and learner access to email

Preparation

1. Establish a date and time when the most learners from the course will be available to participate in a synchronous chat room discussion. Depending on the location and schedules of learners, it may be necessary to plan for two or more Town Hall Meetings.

2. Provide the learners in the course with guidelines for etiquette and participation in the Town Hall Meeting. The guidelines should include the following, although you may want to add or subtract from this list depending on your preferences as the facilitator:

- Each learner in the course will have the opportunity to ask one question during the meetings.

- Each learner will have the option to ask one follow-up question. Follow-up questions should be to clarify responses to the initial question and not to start a new question.

- Learners are not required to ask questions during the activity.

- If time permits, a limited number of additional questions will be discussed after all learners have had an opportunity to participate.

- Only one learner may ask a question at a time.

- Only the host/guest of the Town Hall Meeting responds to the question posted by the learner.

- Any discussion of questions or responses aside from the response provided by the host/guest of the meeting should take place is a separate "private" chat.

- To the extent possible, have your question (and possible follow-up) prepared in a word processing program prior to joining the Town Hall Meeting activity. You can then cut and paste the question into the synchronous chat room when it is your turn to ask a question.

- To facilitate the meeting, learners will ask questions in reverse alphabetical order based on last names (that is, starting with last names that begin with Z and progressing to A).

Note: It is often useful to include in the email the order in which learners will be asking questions; otherwise there may be confusion related to who is to ask the next question.

3. Identify a synchronous chat room for the activity. Most online course delivery tools (for example, Blackboard®, WebCT®, LearningSpace®) offer multiple chat rooms that can be used simultaneously for group activities or alone for whole-class activities. From the available chat rooms, select a specific one (chat room one or chat room A) for the activity.

4. Have a practice chat two days before the activity for learners to verify that they have access.

Process

1. Enter the synchronous chat room at least five to ten minutes prior to the beginning of the Town Hall Meeting.

2. Post a copy of the guidelines for etiquette and participation to the chat room in order to remind learners of the format that is being used for the activity.

3. Identify the first learner who is to ask a question.

4. Have the learner post his or her question.

5. Respond to the question, and then ask if he or she has a follow-up question.

6. Address learners who do not follow the guidelines you have posted (for example, commenting on the question of another learner) and remind them of the guidelines for the activity.

7. Give all learners an opportunity to submit a question (and potentially a follow-up question).

Facilitator Notes

- As an alternative to a second or third Town Hall Meeting, you may choose to permit learners who cannot attend the activity to submit questions by proxy, thus allowing their peers in the course to submit their questions to the group during the meeting. In addition, many synchronous chat software applications will allow the facilitator to record a transcript of the Town Hall Meeting activity that can later be made available to learners who were not able to attend the activity.

- While the activity is designed for the host (that is, the facilitator) to be the respondent to learner questions, you may also use the format to facilitate online guest speakers or panel discussions (for example, panel discussions with learners who have additional experience on a course topic).

53

Point Counterpoint

Activity Summary

By developing controversy and encouraging learners to play the role of "devil's advocate," the Point Counterpoint activity engages learners in almost any asynchronous discussion.

Goals

- Learners will be engaged in an asynchronous discussion with their peers
- Learners will identify alternative perspectives on issues related to the course content
- Learners will develop communication skills for discussing controversial topics in asynchronous discussions

Collaborative Learning

Large groups (all learners in a course)

Recommended e-Learning Experience

Learner—Novice
Facilitator—Novice

Mode

Asynchronous

Time Required

Three to five days (once-a-day minimum learner participation)

Materials

- Facilitator and learner access to an online asynchronous discussion board
- Facilitator and learner access to email

Preparation

1. Select three to five topic statements to be discussed by learners in the course (for example, constitutional rights, role of religion, ethical issues, challenges to longstanding theories and accepted practice). Although controversial topics are not necessary, they can further engage learners in the activity. Some sample topic statements follow:
   - The current role of the federal government in telecommunications is inappropriate for a free marketplace.
   - The influence of religion in education today is unconstitutional.
   - The importance of self-directed learning in distance education has decreased with the use of interactive online technologies.
   - By testing null hypotheses researchers create confusion and miscommunications for readers who are interpreting results.
   - The application of Deming's quality management principles continues to be useful in today's high-tech businesses.
   - Situational Leadership® tactics should be used by all managers within our company.
2. Create a forum for each of the topic statements in the course's asynchronous discussion board.

Process

1. Email learners with instructions to post to the activity discussion forum. Include in the instructions that, whether or not they agree with the required perspective, each posted reply must reflect the opposite perspective on the topic as the previously posted message. For example:

   "All training should be done online."

   Point: "Yes, I agree that all training should be done online."

   Counterpoint: "No, I can't learn without small group discussion, so I disagree that all training should be done online."

   Point: "Online courses often include small group discussions."

   Counterpoint: "Ok, we can have group discussions online, but without the nonverbal cues it is too confusing to be effective."

   Point: "By using acronyms and emoticons we can make up for the missing nonverbal cues and make online discussions very effective."

   Counterpoint: "Even so, it takes the development of several new study skills for people to learn online."

   Point: "I agree, but with the right preparation learners can move to online courses."

2. Encourage learners to play the role of "devil's advocate" and to post responses that may not be representative of their personal perspective on the issue.

3. Participate in the forum discussions, adding point or counterpoint postings when useful for extending the activity and exploring alternative perspectives.

4. End the Point Counterpoint activity when learners can not identify an alternative perspective on the forum's topic statement.

Facilitator Notes

Depending on the number of point and counterpoint postings learners can make on a topic, the length of the activity can vary. For example, on naturally controversial issues (for example, religion, abortion, the death penalty, null hypothesis testing) the Point Counterpoint can inspire many postings by learners and take several days to complete. On less controversial topics (for example, APA or MLA formatting), you may want to create additional forums or reduce the length of the activity.

54

Peer-Moderated Discussions

Activity Summary

The Peer-Moderated Discussions activity can be used to increase the engagement of learners in asynchronous discussions. By offering learners the opportunity to lead discussions, you can gain valuable contributions and strengthen the diversity of discussions, thus allowing peers to establish new and unique directions.

Goals

- Learners will moderate asynchronous discussions within an online course
- Learners will encourage the participation of their peers
- Learners will develop the skills necessary for effectively communicating in asynchronous online discussions

Collaborative Learning

Large groups (all learners in a course)

Recommended e-Learning Experience

Learner—Novice
Facilitator—Novice

Mode

Asynchronous

Time Required

Three to six days (once-a-day minimum learner participation)

Materials

- Facilitator and learner access to an online asynchronous discussion board
- Facilitator and learner access to email

Preparation

1. Select two to four course-related topics for the activity.
2. Create a forum in the course's asynchronous discussion board for each topic.
3. Assign learners to be moderators of topic discussions.

Process

1. Email each learner moderator for the activity with the topic and discussion forum he or she has been assigned. Include in the email any specific topic-related issues that you would like the moderator to include during the activity.
2. Advise the moderators that it is their responsibility to engage their peers in the discussions related to their assigned topics. To begin their discussion area they may want to pose one or more questions related to the topic, or they may start the discussion with controversial statements that can lead to engaging discussions on the topic.
3. Encourage moderators to post additional questions or statements throughout the activity and to contact you if they have questions or concerns.

4. Review the discussions within each forum to ensure that critical topics are being discussed and that information being shared is accurate. If there are problems with the discussion, then you should contact the peer moderator.

Facilitator Notes

As a variation, have moderators select the topics to be discussed within the activity. Although they may select topics that are different from those you would have chosen, the diversity of discussions can often be beneficial and offer unique learning opportunities to those in the course.

55

Online Team Presentations

Activity Summary

Online Team Presentations offers learners an opportunity to study a course-related topic and present their findings to their peers using online technologies. The activity also gives learners the chance to work with their peers as a team in developing the materials to be presented.

Goals

- Learners will work with peers to develop a presentation related to a course topic
- Learners will use online technologies to collaborate on a team presentation
- Learners will facilitate an online presentation in the course

Collaborative Learning

Small groups (three to five learners each)

Recommended e-Learning Experience

Learner—Novice
Facilitator—Novice

Mode

Asynchronous

Time Required

Three to five days (once-a-day minimum learner participation)

Materials

- Facilitator and learner access to an online asynchronous discussion board
- Facilitator and learner access to email
- Learner access to Microsoft PowerPoint®
- (Optional) Learner access to a synchronous chat room

Preparation

1. Assign groups of three to five learners each.
2. Select a course-related topic for each group.
3. Create a forum in the course's asynchronous discussion board for each team.
4. Create a forum in the course's asynchronous discussion board for teams to post their presentations.

Process

1. Email each team with directions for the activity and the contact information for team members.
2. Give the learners three to five days to collaboratively develop a presentation on the assigned topic.
3. Have learners create the presentation using Microsoft PowerPoint. Learners who do not have access to the software should be encouraged to download the free PowerPoint Viewer.

4. Require that team presentations include ten or more Power-Point slides, as well as content for communicating important concepts within the course (for example, background literature, key factors for success, references, additional resources, supporting data).

5. Have each team post its completed presentation as an attachment to the designated discussion forum.

6. Encourage learners to view the presentations of their peers and to discuss the topics presented in the discussion forum.

Facilitator Notes

- Online presentations can also be done using many synchronous chat room tools. If these capabilities are available for your online course, then learners can provide "real time" narration for their presentation slides in the synchronous chat room as their peers view each slide.

- Depending on the technology capabilities of learners within the course, you may or may not want to encourage learners to attach audio files to their team presentations. While these can offer an interactive and engaging element to team presentations, the ability for all learners in the course to access the audio narration may be restricted by Internet bandwidth limitations. If audio narrations are not to be included, teams can use text narrations to facilitate presentations and provide learners with information related to the assigned course topics.

56

Peer-Pair Feedback

Activity Summary

Having learners in an online course provide Peer-Pair Feedback can be a valuable tool for building online communities, engaging learners in an interactive environment, and managing the amount of individualized feedback that is often required for effective instruction.

Goals

- Learners will work with partners to review course-related assignments
- Learners will provide their peer partners with feedback on drafts of their assignments
- Learners will build skills for effectively providing constructive criticism to peers in online courses

Collaborative Learning

Pairs of learners

Recommended e-Learning Experience

Learner—Novice
Facilitator—Novice

Mode

Asynchronous

Time Required

Two to three days (once-a-day minimum learner participation)

Materials

Facilitator and learner access to email.

Preparation

1. Select an assignment for the course in which learners would benefit from having peer feedback before submitting a final version.

2. Assign learners to partners for the activity.

3. Develop a list of feedback comments that learners should use in reviewing the draft assignments that will be submitted by their peer-pair partners. Sample feedback comments that may be useful include:

Reviewer's name:

Reviewer's email:

Name of assignment:

Assignment received from:

Date received for review:

Date reviewed and emailed back:

On a scale of 1 to 10 rate the following (with 10 being ideal):

- Grammar and spelling:
- Formatting:
- Readability (flow of content):
- Use of illustrations and graphics:

Identify two or more elements of the assignment that exceeded your expectations:

Identify two or more elements of the assignment that did not exceed your expectations:

At least two specific suggestions for improving the assignment:

Other comments:

Process

1. Email each learner with instructions for the activity, the email address of his or her peer-pair partner, and your list of required feedback comments.

2. Have learners complete a draft of an assignment for the course (for example, a literature review, final report, analysis findings report, or presentation).

3. Have learners email copies of the draft assignment as an attachment to their Peer-Pair Feedback partners.

4. Require peer-pair partners for the activity to complete the feedback comments for their partners' draft assignment, encouraging learners to offer both useful comments and constructive criticism.

5. Have learners email the completed feedback comments to their partners.

6. Direct learners to make the necessary adjustments to their assignment based on the feedback of their peer-pair partners.

7. Require each learner to include with his or her final assignment a copy of the feedback he or she received from the partner as well as a short (one- to two-paragraph) description of the changes he or she made to the draft based on the feedback.

Facilitator Notes

- The Peer-Pair Feedback activity can also be done with small groups of three to five learners. As a group activity, learners should use a round-robin format where Learner A submits a draft assignment to Leaner B, Learner B submits to Learner C, and Learner C submits to Learner A.

- Depending on the scope of the assignment, you may also encourage peer-pairs to complete more than one round of reviews, thereby providing feedback on a series of draft assignments before a final product is submitted.

- If you use the Peer-Pair Feedback activity early in a course, then learners may also work with their partners in providing peer feedback on later assignments without the structured activity.

57

Guest Speaker Press Conference

Activity Summary

A Guest Speaker Press Conference is an informal format for promoting interactions among learners and guest speakers. Like press conferences that follow sporting events or new events, the questions asked by learners during this activity are spontaneous and build upon the previous questions.

Goals

- Learners will provide input and discussion related to ground rules that will be used to facilitate online course dialogues
- Learners will agree on policies for managing synchronous and/or asynchronous online discussions
- Learners will build online communication skills

Collaborative Learning

Large groups (all learners in a course)

Recommended e-Learning Experience

Learner—Moderate
Facilitator—Moderate
Guest speaker—Moderate

Mode

Synchronous and Asynchronous

Time Required

90 to 120 minutes

Materials

- Facilitator, guest, and learner access to an online asynchronous discussion board
- Facilitator, guest, and learner access to an online synchronous chat room

Preparation

1. Identify a guest speaker for the course.
2. Determine a date and time when the greatest number of learners in the course can participate in a synchronous conversation with the guest speaker.
3. Develop guidelines for etiquette and participation. The guidelines should include the following, although you may want to add or subtract from this list:

- Review the required readings and other information related to the guest speaker prior to the press conference
- Visit the synchronous chat area of the course the day before the activity to ensure that you have the necessary software applications to fully participate in the discussion (for example, new versions of Web browser software, plug-ins)
- Create a good study environment for the activity (turn off email, instant messengers, television, and other distracters)
- Arrive to the activity at least five minutes early

- Do not greet the other participants when you arrive or when they arrive

- Address your questions or comments to the guest speaker (for example, "Dr. Phillips, can you explain that concept again?")

- When possible, cut and paste questions that you prepared prior to the Guest Speaker Press Conference activity into the synchronous chat instead of typing them in at the time

- "Raise your hand" to gain the attention of the guest speaker by posting a blank message. The guest speaker will identify which learner can post the next question from the list of those who have posted blank messages

- Avoid sarcasm, idioms, slang, jargon, and other statements that may lead to miscommunications

- Leave misspelled words unless the error changes the meaning of the message

- The press conference will begin with a short introduction provided by the facilitator and a brief statement to be provided by the guest speaker. Following their presentation you may ask questions that you have for the guest speaker. Your questions may be spontaneous or planned ahead of time, and you may ask follow-up questions if the guest speaker chooses

- Following the press conference, post a newspaper-like description of the key points you learned during the activity

4. Create a forum in the course's asynchronous discussion board.

5. Identify a synchronous chat room for the activity. Most online course delivery tools (Blackboard®, WebCT®, LearningSpace®) offer multiple chat rooms that can be used simultaneously for group activities or alone for whole-class activities. From the available chat rooms, select a specific chat room (chat room one or chat room A) for the activity.

6. Have a practice chat two days before the Guest Speaker Press Conference activity for learners to verify that they have access.

7. Write a short introduction to the guest expert in your word processing program.

Process

1. Welcome the expert to the synchronous chat room by cutting and pasting a short introduction from the word processing program into the synchronous chat room.

2. Have the guest speaker select which learners should post the next question in the chat room. Learners can indicate their interest in asking a question by posting a blank message.

3. Keep an eye on the time and let the learners and guest speaker know when there are ten minutes left in the Guest Speaker Press Conference activity.

4. End the synchronous chat on time, and thank everyone for their participation.

5. Have each learner post to the asynchronous discussion forum a newspaper-like description of what occurred and what he or she learned during the press conference.

6. Post a copy of the transcripts from the synchronous chat, if available, to the asynchronous forum.

Facilitator Notes

- Because a Guest Speaker Press Conference is informal and relatively unstructured, this activity is most effective when you, as the facilitator, don't have specific objectives that must be achieved through the activity. You may also want to encourage participants to use emoticons and acronyms as informal communication techniques during the activity.

- Guest speakers for the activity can be learners from within the course. In almost any course there are individual learners who are knowledgeable in one or more subject areas closely related to the course topic. You can ask these learners to hold press conferences, offering peers in the course the opportunity to learn from the experiences of their fellow learners.

- The Guest Speaker Press Conference activity can also be done using asynchronous discussion boards. Although this requires a longer commitment of time by the guest speaker, it can be easier to manage for learners and guest speakers with only novice levels of e-learning experience.

58

....

Answers[2]

Activity Summary

The Answers[2] activity utilizes peer teams to extend, improve, or develop answers to case-based questions related to course content. You may use this activity to promote collaborative learning and build critical thinking skills.

Goals

- Learners will answer case-based question(s) related to course materials
- Learners will work with their peers to identify the synergies among their answers and make improvements
- Learners will build skills for interacting with other learners in the course

Collaborative Learning

Small groups (2 or 4 learners each)

Recommended e-Learning Experience

Learner—Novice
Facilitator—Novice

Mode

Asynchronous

Time Required

Three to five days (once-a-day minimum learner participation)

Materials

- Facilitator and learner access to an online asynchronous discussion board
- Facilitator and learner access to email

Preparation

1. Identify one or more case-based questions that are related to the course content. The questions for the activity do not have to be complete case studies; instead they can be shorter questions that simply provide a small amount of context for the questions. Below are two examples:

    Sample Question A: You are a computer systems trainer at a large national bank, and Isaiah is a bank teller at a regional branch of your organization. During a training course on using the newest computer system, you discuss that all of the organization's computers utilize virus protection software. At the next break, Isaiah asks you to explain the common threats to financial computer systems.

    Sample Question B: Rhonda is a salesperson for the organization in which you are the human resources director. Two months ago Rhonda filed a sexual harassment complaint against her supervisor. Although the specific case is still under review, you are scheduled to give a sexual harassment presentation tomorrow to the division in which Rhonda works. What topics do you include in your agenda for the presentation?

2. Create collaborative teams of two or four learners each.

3. Assign a case-based question to each collaborative team. You can use the same question for all teams of learners or assign unique questions for each team.

4. Create a forum in the course's asynchronous discussion board for each team.

5. Create a forum in the course's asynchronous discussion board for each team's collaborative response to the case-based questions.

Process

1. Email instructions for the activity to each learner, including the assigned case-based question and the names of the other learners in the assigned teams.

2. Require each learner to first answer the case-based question on his or her own before participating with peers in the activity.

3. Have each learner post his or her answer to the case-based question to the discussion forum.

4. Instruct the collaborative teams to develop a single answer to the case-based question.

5. Have each collaborative team post the team's response to the case-based question to the designated discussion forum.

Facilitator Notes

- As an alternative to assigning just one question to each team of learners, use multiple questions and assign all of the questions to each of the teams. Each learner would then answer several questions, and in turn each team would come to agreement on a single answer to each question using the input of all of the team members.

- The activity can also be done using synchronous chat rooms.

59

Collaborative Concept Maps

Activity Summary

The creation of concept maps can be a useful technique for visualizing the relationships among topics, issues, and themes in an online course. The Collaborative Concept Maps activity engages teams of learners in the development of concept maps that can then be shared with their peers as study aids for the course.

Goals

- Learners will identify significant relationships among key topics, issues, or themes from the course
- Learners will work together to create a concept map of key topics, issues, or themes from the course
- Learners will build skills for communicating effectively online using both text and visual elements

Collaborative Learning

Small groups (3 to 5 learners each)

Recommended e-Learning Experience

Learner—Advanced
Facilitator—Advanced

Mode

Asynchronous

Time Required

Three to five days (once-a-day minimum learner participation)

Materials

- Facilitator and learner access to an online asynchronous discussion board
- Facilitator and learner access to email
- Learner access to Microsoft Word® or PowerPoint®

Preparation

1. Assign learners to collaborative learning teams of three to five members each.
2. Create a forum in the course's asynchronous discussion board for each collaborative team.
3. Create a forum in the course's asynchronous discussion board for the Collaborative Concept Maps from each team.

Process

1. Email learners instructions for the activity.
2. Have each learner identify ten or more key topics, issues, or themes from the course.
3. Have each learner post his or her list of key topics, issues, and themes from the course to the collaborative team's discussion forum.
4. Require each learner to review all of the topics, issues, or themes identified by team members before recommending relationships among the topics, issues, and themes for the Collaborative Concept Map.
5. Have collaborative teams create concept maps that illustrate the relationship of ten or more key topics, issues, and themes from the course in a single diagram.

Using Microsoft Word or PowerPoint learners can create and edit concept maps by using the Text Box option found on the Drawing toolbar. Individual text boxes can be generated for each key topic, issue, and theme identified by the learners. Using the Arrow and Line functions, also found on the Drawing toolbar, learners can identify relationships among the topics, issues, and themes.

6. Require each team to post in the designated discussion forum as an attachment one Collaborative Concept Map representing the key topics, issues, and themes identified by the team members, as well as relationships among the elements.

7. Encourage learners to review the Collaborative Concept Maps of their peers and to use these as study aids for the course.

Facilitator Notes

- If available, collaborative teams may also use concept mapping software such as Microsoft Visio® or Inspiration® for the activity. If teams use specialized software, it is useful for all team members to have a copy of the software, and for the final Collaborative Concept Maps to be saved as HTML or PDF files to ensure that all learners in the course can view the illustrations.

- For online courses with fewer than ten learners, use the Collaborative Concept Maps activity as an individual activity.

60

Group Blogs

Activity Summary

Blogs are the online (or Web) equivalent of journals, and the Group Blogs activity engages learners in the development of a collaborative blog throughout an online course. Somewhere between a "diary" and "course logbook," the blog captures the important learning experiences and educational activities of a course in a format that can be used as a tool for reviewing course materials or reflecting on learning.

Goals

- Learners will collaborate with their group members in the development of a blog
- Learners will reflect on their learning experiences
- Learners will create a blog of the online course experience
- Learners will build skills for interacting online with their peers

Collaborative Learning

Medium groups (8 to 15 learners each)

Recommended e-Learning Experience

Learner—Novice
Facilitator—Novice

Mode
Asynchronous

Time Required
Ongoing task throughout the course

Materials
- Facilitator and learner access to an online asynchronous discussion board
- Facilitator and learner access to email

Preparation
1. Form collaborative groups of eight to fifteen learners each.
2. Create a forum in the course's asynchronous discussion board for each collaborative group.

Process
1. Email learners at the beginning of the course with the instructions for the Group Blogs activity and the names of other learners assigned to the collaborative groups.
2. Require that each collaborative group have at least one entry every other day throughout the duration of the course. No single learner has to contribute every second day, but one group member must contribute an entry to the blog at least every other day.
3. Have learners include in their blog entries any thoughts, comments, perceptions, ideas, suggestions, feelings, or accomplishments that they would like to share with their peers in the course. There should be no "right" or "wrong" blog entries, although learners should be aware that blog entries are not confidential. Blog entries can include:

- Let me explain in plain language. . .
- If I were describing this to a fifth grader. . .
- My understanding is. . .
- The net effect or impact of this is. . .
- Let me say it in a different way. . .
- This makes sense because. . .
- If I were describing this to my father/mother. . .
- I was shocked because. . .
- To illustrate my understanding. . .

4. Encourage learners in each collaborative group to assign a schedule of entry dates for each group member.

5. Have learners review the blog at the end of the course and summarize what they have learned through the course experience.

Facilitator Notes

- Individuals can also keep blogs (or journals) in a course. As an individual activity you may require fewer entries each week to the blog.

- As an alternative, assign a single blog that all learners can contribute to during the course. This can be especially useful for online courses with fewer than fifteen learners.

- Blogs can also focus on specific course topics, issues, or themes. For example, you may assign a group to keep a blog just on the leadership issues discussed in the course, while another group maintains a blog on the legal implications of topics discussed in the course.

Peer Quizzes

Activity Summary

The Peer Quizzes activity is a useful exercise for learners to review course materials, to self-assess their learning and/or to prepare for an evaluation. By involving all learners in the development of quiz items, you can improve learner engagement, develop collaborative study groups, review course materials, and build online community.

Goals

- Learners will reflect on course content and materials
- Learners will contribute one or more quiz items
- Learners will self-assess their learning

Collaborative Learning

Large groups (all learners in a course)

Recommended e-Learning Experience

Learner—Novice
Facilitator—Novice

Mode

Asynchronous

Time Required

Two to three days (once-a-day minimum learner participation)

Materials

- Facilitator and learner access to an online asynchronous discussion board
- Facilitator and learner access to email

Preparation

1. Create a forum in the course's asynchronous discussion board for learners to post quiz items.
2. Create a forum in the course's asynchronous discussion board for learners to post answers to their quiz items.

Process

1. Email learners with instructions for the activity.
2. Require each learner to contribute at least one quiz item related to course content to the designated discussion forum. When a quiz item has been posted, duplicate items cannot be submitted by other learners.
3. Require learners to post the answers to their quiz item(s) in the designated discussion forum.
4. Encourage all learners to review each quiz item and the corresponding correct answer. These items can be used by learners to review for quizzes or tests or in preparation for other course assignments.

Facilitator Notes

Depending on the number of learners in the course, you may want to require learners to post more than one quiz item.

20 Questions

Activity Summary

The 20 Questions game is a wonderful exercise for engaging learners and increasing their participation in almost any online course. You can use 20 Questions to develop online communities within the course.

Goals

- Learners will collaborate with their group members in developing twenty questions
- Learners will interact online in order to meet other learners in the course
- Learners will build skills for interacting online with their peers

Collaborative Learning

Small groups (three to five groups in total)

Recommended e-Learning Experience

Learner—Novice
Facilitator—Novice

Mode

Asynchronous

Time Required

Three to six days (once-a-day minimum learner participation)

Materials

- Facilitator and learner access to an online asynchronous discussion board
- Facilitator and learner access to email

Preparation

1. Form three to five collaborative groups.
2. Create a forum in the course's asynchronous discussion board for each collaborative group.
3. Identify a course-related historical person or commonly used item (for example, in a science course with five learners, you could choose Einstein, Newton, funnel, thermometer, and beaker; or in a computer course, you could choose hard drive, floppy disk, CD-ROM, Bill Gates, and Charles Babbage).

Process

1. Email learners the instructions for the activity as well as the names of learners in their collaborative groups.
2. Inform collaborative groups that as a team they are to only email you a total of twenty questions in order to identify the person or item that you have selected. Group members should work together in the discussion forum to identify useful and appropriate questions to ask. All questions must be answerable with one of the following responses: yes, no, irrelevant, probably, doubtful, sometimes, usually, rarely, or unknown.

3. Require each collaborative group to identify one learner to be the individual who will email you questions from that group and post your responses to the group's discussion forum.

4. Respond to as many as twenty questions emailed to you by each collaborative group. Each response should be limited to a one-word answer. Your responses may include the following:

Yes—You are sure about your answer of Yes.

No—You are sure about your answer of No.

Irrelevant—The question does not apply to your object.

Probably—You are not sure but you think the answer might be Yes.

Doubtful—You are not sure but you think the answer might be No.

Sometimes—Sometimes Yes, sometimes No.

Usually—Most of the time, the answer would be Yes.

Rarely—Most of the time, the answer would be No.

Unknown—You are unsure of how the question relates or you don't know. These questions do not count against a group's twenty.

5. Have collaborative groups email you when they believe that they have identified the historical person or commonly used item that you have selected.

6. Congratulate groups when they have identified the correct historical person or commonly used item.

Facilitator Notes

- The 20 Questions game can also be facilitated using a synchronous chat room, although the activity works better as an individual exercise when using this technology.
- Another variation of the 20 Questions activity is Who or What Am I? (see activity 10).

63

Online with Socrates

Activity Summary

The Online with Socrates activity brings the Socratic method of teaching to online courses. By using questions, as a facilitator you can guide learners through complex course materials while building their self-confidence, keeping them engaged in the discussion, and improving skills for independent and critical thinking.

Goals

- Learners will collaborate with their group members in answering questions posed by the instructor
- Learners will engage in the learning experience through small-group and whole-class discussions
- Learners will build skills for interacting online with their peers

Collaborative Learning

Small groups (three to five groups total)

Recommended e-Learning Experience

Learner—Moderate
Facilitator—Advanced

Mode

Synchronous

Time Required

60 to 90 minutes

Materials

- Facilitator and learner access to multiple online synchronous chat rooms
- Facilitator and learner access to email

Preparation

1. Form three to five collaborative groups.
2. Determine a date and time when the greatest number of learners in the course can participate in a synchronous activity.
3. Identify three to five unique chat rooms, one for each of the collaborative groups.
4. Identify a primary chat room for discussions among all collaborative groups.
5. Prepare a list of questions related to the course's content. Unlike items for a quiz or test, the questions should not be in random order. Rather, the questions should lead to the discussion of important topics, issues, or themes in the course. Socratic questions:
   - Keep the discussion focused
   - Stimulate further discussion
   - Periodically summarize the discussion
   - Engage learners in the discussion

   Below are some sample Socratic questions:
   - Do you know what's happening to the rain forests in South America?
   - How do you know that they are getting smaller?

- What evidence supports your answer?
- Are you saying that you learned about the rain forests from the nightly news?
- If scientists have reported to the media that the rain forests are getting smaller, how do they know that?
- How long have scientists been studying the size of the rain forests?

Process

1. Email learners with instructions for the activity, including the date, time, chat room location for the activity, and their assigned collaborative groups.
2. Have all learners in the course initially enter the primary chat room.
3. Post the initial Socratic question from your list to begin the activity.
4. Give each collaborative group five minutes to discuss the question and possible answers in their assigned chat room.
5. Have each group present its answer to the question in the primary chat room.
6. Respond to the group answers either by posting a follow-up question related to their answers or by posting a new question from your list.
7. Give each collaborative group five minutes to discuss the new question and possible answers in their assigned chat room.
8. Repeat the process throughout the duration of the activity, asking questions in the primary chat room, providing five minutes for discussion in the individual group chat rooms, having each group post its answers in the primary chat room, and asking another question based on the group answers.

Facilitator Notes

- The Online with Socrates activity can also be done using only forums in the course's asynchronous discussion board. You should anticipate five to seven days to complete the activity asynchronously.

- If you do not have access to multiple chat rooms for the course, have collaborative groups discuss the Socratic questions in asynchronous discussion forums and then post their groups' responses in the synchronous chat room. You may want to provide eight to ten minutes for discussion when using this variation.

64

In the Hot Seat

Activity Summary

As an exercise to build collaborative relationships among online learners, the In the Hot Seat activity can be used in almost any online course. During the activity, groups of learners will prepare resources and review course materials in order to answer questions submitted by their peers on the day that their group is In the Hot Seat.

Goals

- Learners will collaborate to answer questions posted by their peers
- Learners will reflect on their learning experiences in preparation for the activity
- Learners will build skills for interacting online with their peers

Collaborative Learning

Small groups (3 to 5 learners each)

Recommended e-Learning Experience

Learner—Novice
Facilitator—Novice

Mode

Asynchronous

Time Required

One day for each collaborative group (once-a-day minimum learner participation)

Materials

- Facilitator and learner access to an online asynchronous discussion board
- Facilitator and learner access to email

Preparation

1. Assign learners to collaborative groups of three to five learners each.

2. Assign each collaborative group to a topic, issue, or theme from the course.

3. Assign each collaborative group to a day (a 24-hour period) when the course will focus on their topic, issue, or theme (for example, the first Tuesday of Module Three).

4. Create a single forum in the course's asynchronous discussion board that will be used by each of the collaborative groups on their assigned day to be In the Hot Seat.

5. Email learners in the course with their group assignments and their groups' assigned course topics, issues, or themes a few days before the activity is to begin.

6. Have learners gather resources, study, and prepare to answer questions that other learners in the course may have on the day that their group is In the Hot Seat.

Process

1. Send an email informing learners of the schedule for the In the Hot Seat activity (on which day(s) during the course they will be able to ask questions of the assigned collaborative groups). For example, "On the first Tuesday of Module Three you will be able to ask questions related to Internet copyright laws in the course's asynchronous discussion forum."

2. Have learners post questions that they have regarding the current topic, issue, or theme to the discussion forum on the day that their peers' collaborative group has been assigned.

3. Require learners in the assigned collaborative group to answer the questions posted by their peers throughout the day that their group is In the Hot Seat.

4. Monitor the questions and responses throughout the day while a group is In the Hot Seat, verifying that the answers given are accurate and useful.

Facilitator Notes

You can also assign individuals to be In the Hot Seat if you are teaching an online course with fewer than ten to fifteen learners.

65

Round Robin

Activity Summary

The Round Robin activity is an effective technique for getting all of the learners in a course to generate a shared knowledge base on a course topic. Using only email, the activity can actively engage all learners in the course and build online community even when other synchronous and asynchronous technologies are not available.

Goals

- Learners will collaborate with their peers in building a common knowledge base
- Learners will review their understanding of course topics, issues, or themes
- Learners will use email to interact online with their peers

Collaborative Learning

Large groups (all learners in a course)

Recommended e-Learning Experience

Learner—Novice
Facilitator—Novice

Mode

Asynchronous

Time Required

Two to three days (once-a-day minimum learner participation)

Materials

Facilitator and learner access to email

Preparation

1. Identify two to three important course topics, issues, or themes.

2. Create an ordered list of learners in the course, including email addresses, for example, alphabetical, reverse alphabetical, random, by birthdays, by division or department.

3. Include your name and email address as the last person on the list.

Process

1. Email the first learner on the list with the name of the topic, issue, or theme you selected (for example, computer security, Situational Leadership®, Napoleon, or South Africa).

2. Include with the email the ordered list of learners for the activity.

3. Require the first learner on the list to add one additional piece of information related to the topic, issue, or theme (for example, virus protection software enhances computer security; the French people both loved and hated Napoleon).

4. Have the first learner forward the email, now containing both the topic you identified and the additional information, to the next learner on the list.

5. Require each subsequent learner on the list to add one additional piece of information related to the topic, issue, or theme that you identified before forwarding the message on to the next learner (for example, firewalls are also essential tools for computer security; Napoleon was exiled from France on more than one occasion).

6. Email the complete Round Robin to all learners in the course when the email message returns to you. If a learner cannot identify any additional information to add to the topic, issue, or theme, then he or she should send you the message and request a new topic. That person will then become the first learner on the list to add information to the new topic, issue, or theme that you identify.

Facilitator Notes

When a Round Robin is complete (that is, a message that you started has been added to by all learners in the course), either start a new Round Robin or have the first learner on the list identify the topic, issue, or theme to be the focus of the second Round Robin.

66

Team Peer Reviews

Activity Summary

Having collaborative groups in an online course provide Team Peer Reviews can be a valuable tool for building online communities, engaging learners in an interactive course environment, and managing the amount of feedback that is often required for effective instruction.

Goals

- Collaborative teams will develop group assignments
- Collaborative teams will review and provide peer reviews to other groups in the course on course-related assignments
- Learners will build skills for effectively providing constructive criticism to peers in online courses

Collaborative Learning

Small groups (3 to 5 learners each)

Recommended e-Learning Experience

Learner—Moderate
Facilitator—Moderate

Mode

Asynchronous

Time Required

Six or more days (once-a-day minimum learner participation)

Materials

- Facilitator and learner access to an online asynchronous discussion board
- Facilitator and learner access to email

Preparation

1. Select a team or small-group project in which collaborative groups would benefit from having peer feedback before submitting a final version.
2. Create collaborative groups of three to five learners each.
3. Assign team pairs for the activity (Team A and Team D, Team B and Team C).
4. Develop a list of feedback comments that teams should use in reviewing the draft assignments that will be submitted by their peer teams. Examples of comments that may be useful include the following:

Names of reviewers:

Name of assignment:

Assignment received from:

Date received for review:

Date reviewed and emailed back:

On a scale of 1 to 10 rate the following (with 10 being ideal):

- Grammar and spelling:
- Formatting:
- Readability (flow of content):
- Use of illustrations and graphics:

Identify two or more elements of the assignment that exceeded your team's expectations:

Identify two or more elements of the assignment that did not exceed your team's expectations:

At least two specific suggestions for improving the assignment:

Other comments:

5. Create a forum in the course's asynchronous discussion board for each team.

6. Post in each forum a copy of the feedback comments.

7. Create a separate forum in the course's asynchronous discussion board for the sharing of team assignments.

Process

1. Email all learners in the course with instructions for the activity and the discussion forum location for their teams.

2. Have each team complete a draft of its small-group assignment for the course (for example, annotated Webliography, research report, analysis findings report, or presentation). Teams can use email and their discussion forum to develop and finalize their assignments.

3. Have each team post a copy of its assignment to the shared discussion forum for their partner team to download and review.

4. Require all members of the partner teams for the activity to complete the feedback comments for the draft assignment of the team that they were assigned, encouraging learners to offer both useful comments and constructive criticism. Individual team members should each review and provide feedback separately.

5. Have learners post the completed feedback comments to the partner team's discussion forum.

6. Direct teams to make the necessary adjustments to their assignments based on the feedback received from their peers.

7. Review the posted feedback in each team's discussion forum when assessing the assignment.

Facilitator Notes

Depending on the scope of the assignment, encourage teams to complete more than one round of reviews, thereby providing feedback on a series of draft assignments before a final product is submitted.

67

Track Changes

Activity Summary

Assessing the performance of individual learners in small-group projects is challenging both in the traditional classroom as well as in online courses. The Track Changes activity utilizes the capabilities of today's powerful word processing software applications (specifically, Microsoft Word®) to assist learners in communicating more effectively within online teams and to aid facilitators in assessing the individual performance of team members.

Goals

- Learners will collaborate with their group members to complete an assignment
- Learners will keep a record of their contributions to a team assignment
- Learners will review the comments and edits of their team members

Collaborative Learning

Small groups (3 to 5 learners each)

Recommended e-Learning Experience

Learner—Moderate
Facilitator—Moderate

Mode

Asynchronous

Time Required

Three to six days (once-a-day minimum learner participation)

Materials

- Facilitator and learner access to email
- Facilitator and learner access to Microsoft Word

Preparation

1. Select a team or small-group project that requires a written report as its final product.
2. Assign collaborative groups of three to five learners each.

Process

1. Email learners with the collaborative group assignments as well as the names and email addresses of their group members.

2. Inform each collaborative group that they must complete the assignment collaborating only in Microsoft Word in developing the final product.

3. Have each group elect a learner to start the first draft document that will be used as the basis for the final report.

4. Have the selected learner begin a Microsoft Word document for the final product, turning on the Track Changes option from within the Tools menu in Word. The Track Changes feature will allow all collaborative team members, and you in the end, to view the comments, additions, subtractions, and other changes made by group members throughout the development of the report. The comments, additions, subtractions, and other changes will be color coded automatically by Microsoft Word.

5. Have the initial learner then email the Word file to another team member for him or her to add comments, edits, or other changes to the report.

6. Inform each group that when they have collaborated on the final product for the assignment they should include in the Word document a list of the team members, along with the color assigned to each individual's comments and edits (for example, Nathan Robins = Blue). Using the Reviewing menu bar in Microsoft Word®, learners can select the Show option in order to access a list of reviewers and their assigned colors. Changes to the color options can also be made using these menu options.

7. Have each group email you a copy of their final report with the Track Changes feature still turned on and visible.

Facilitator Notes

- You can also use the Track Changes feature to facilitate peer feedback on assignments and activities (see Peer-Pair Feedback, activity 56).

- Track Changes can also be used by you, as the facilitator, to provide individualized feedback on activities and assignments completed in Microsoft Word. After turning on the feature and making your comments, simply save the file and send it back to the learner (or collaborative group).

68

Presidential Debate

Activity Summary

The Presidential Debate format can be extremely useful for communicating with a large number of online learners in structured synchronous discussion. By offering learners an organized forum for asking questions on course-related topics, this activity can remove the confusion that often accompanies unstructured synchronous discussions.

Goals

- Learners will participate in synchronous discussions with their peers
- Learners will have the opportunity to ask questions and discuss issues as a group
- Learners will build skills necessary for effective online synchronous discussions

Collaborative Learning

Large groups (all learners in a course)

Recommended e-Learning Experience

Learner—Moderate
Facilitator—Moderate

Mode

Synchronous

Time Required

75 to 90 minutes

Materials

- Facilitator and learner access to a synchronous chat room
- Facilitator and learner access to email

Preparation

1. Establish a date and time when the largest number of learners from the course will be available to participate in a synchronous chat room discussion. Depending on the location and schedules of learners, it may be necessary to plan for two or more Presidential Debates.

2. Identify three to five learners from the course to be participants (candidates) in the debate.

3. Select one or more topics, issues, or themes from the course to focus on during the debate.

4. Provide the learners in the course with guidelines for etiquette and participation in the Presidential Debate. The guidelines should include the following, although you may want to add or subtract from this list depending on your preferences as the facilitator:

   - All learners in the course will have the opportunity to submit one or more questions (related to identified course topics, issues, or themes) to the facilitator prior to the debate.

   - The facilitator will ask all the questions during the debate and direct questions to a specific candidate (that is, learners selected to participate in the debate).

- All learners (other than the three to five selected to participate as candidates for the debate) are required to submit one question prior the activity.

- If time permits, a limited number of additional questions can be submitted to the facilitator as follow-up questions.

- Addressed candidates (participants) in the debate will do their best to quickly and accurately answer questions.

- Any discussion of questions or responses aside from the responses provided by the candidates should take place in a separate "private" chat.

5. Identify a synchronous chat room for the activity. Most online course delivery tools (Blackboard®, WebCT®, Learning-Space®) offer multiple chat rooms that can be used simultaneously for group activities or alone for whole-class activities. From the available chat rooms, select a specific chat room (chat room one or chat room A) for the activity.

6. Have a practice chat two days before the activity for learners to verify that they have access.

Process

1. Have each learner in the course identify at least one question he or she would like to ask related to course topics, issues, or themes.

2. Prioritize questions for the debate and identify which learners will receive which questions.

3. Send a copy of the questions to each candidate in the debate twenty-four hours in advance so each can prepare his or her response.

4. Enter the synchronous chat room at least five to ten minutes prior to the beginning of the Presidential Debate.

5. Post a copy of the guidelines for etiquette and participation to the chat room in order to remind learners of the format that is being used for the activity.

6. Ask the first question of the debate to a specific candidate.

7. Have the candidate answer the question to the best of his or her ability.

8. Clarify any inaccurate or misleading information that the learner may have included in his or her response.

9. Ask the second question you identified from those submitted by learners in the course.

10. Repeat until all of the previously submitted questions are asked, or until time runs out for the activity.

Facilitator Notes

- As an alternative, you may elect not to send a copy of the questions to the candidates in the debate prior to the synchronous chat.

- Asynchronous variations of this activity can also be quite effective in online courses where synchronous discussions are not feasible.

Online Office Hours

Activity Summary

Even in courses that rely primarily on asynchronous communication tools (email, discussion boards), learners can often benefit from the opportunity to interact with their course facilitator and peers through non-required Online Office Hours. Based on the familiar practice at colleges and universities, online facilitators can be available in a synchronous chat room to address learner comments, questions, or concerns.

Goals

- Learners will have the opportunity to interact synchronously with their course facilitator and peers
- Learners will have the opportunity to ask questions and receive timely responses
- Learners will build communication skills for online synchronous discussions

Collaborative Learning

Medium groups (8 to 15 learners each)

Recommended e-Learning Experience

Learner—Novice
Facilitator—Novice

Mode

Synchronous

Time Required

60 to 90 minutes

Materials

Facilitator and learner access to a synchronous chat room

Preparation

1. Identify times during the course when you can be available for "live" (synchronous) Online Office Hours. For example, Monday nights at 8:00 p.m. Mountain Time or Thursday mornings at 10:00 a.m. Eastern Time.
2. Identify a chat room for the activity.
3. Inform learners in the course of the regularly scheduled times for the Online Office Hours. The activity is most useful as an optional resource for learners, with no participation required.

Process

1. Enter the chat room at least five minutes prior to the scheduled time for the Online Office Hours.
2. Have any learner who attend the office hours post a blank message indicating that he or she has a question.
3. Have each learner post questions to the chat room only after you have indicated that it is his or her turn to ask a question.
4. Respond to learner questions promptly.

Facilitator Notes

For courses with more than fifteen learners or learners in various time zones, you may want to establish multiple Online Office Hours to ensure that everyone has an opportunity to participate.

70

Online Jigsaw Learning*

Activity Summary

Online Jigsaw Learning offers e-learners the unique opportunity to interact in the online environment as both learners and peer-instructors, while offering instructors a useful tool for reducing the time required to cover a large amount of course material. As an alternative to online group presentations, this activity utilizes course materials that can be divided in independent "chunks" or "segments" to facilitate study groups and peer-instruction.

Goals

- Learners will study course content related to their assigned "chunk" of course materials
- Learners will provide instruction to the peers in their group on the "chunk" of course materials they were assigned
- Learners will work collaboratively to study course content
- Learners will build skills necessary for effective online asynchronous discussions

Collaborative Learning

Individual and small group (3 to 6 learners)

---

*Developed in collaboration with Mel Silberman. See Silberman and Lawson (1995) for a traditional classroom version of the activity.

Recommended e-Learning Experience

Learner—Moderate

Facilitator—Moderate

Mode

Asynchronous

Time Required

Three to six days (once-a-day minimum learner participation)

Materials

- Instructor and learner access to an online asynchronous discussion board
- Instructor and learner access to email
- (Optional) Instructor and learner access to a synchronous chat room

Preparation

1. Analyze and divide the course content into three to six "chunks" or "segments." For example, if you are teaching a course on the types of legal structures for a business, you may divide the content into four "chunks," including S corporations, partnerships, sole proprietorships, and limited liability partnerships (or five "chunks" if you include C corporations).

2. Identify resources learners will use during the activity (texts, articles, readings, websites, etc.).

3. Assign learners to Online Jigsaw Learning groups of three to six learners depending on the number of "chunks" (there should be one chunk for each learner in a group).

4. Assign each jigsaw learning group a case-based question(s) to respond to. Two case-based question examples follow:

- "As the owner/manager of a small retail store that has six employees, you have decided that it is time to open two additional stores in regional shopping centers. Before opening the additional stores, you would like to more formally establish your business as a corporation. What are the advantages and disadvantages of the legal structures available to you?"

- "The law firm that you work for has many clients who are looking to start up new businesses and asking about the advantages to alternative legal structures for their growing organizations. As a result, your group has been asked to create a decision tree or algorithm that can be used by lawyers in your firm to quickly assess the available and appropriate legal structures for each of these clients."

5. Create a forum in the course's asynchronous discussion board for each jigsaw learning group.

Process

1. Email learners with directions for the activity and the "chunk" of course material they have been assigned (that is, learner A is assigned S Corporations and learner B is assigned Sole Proprietorships). In addition, you can provide a list of the primary resources learners should use in completing the activity (specific texts, articles, readings, or websites) as well as a list of supplemental or optional resources, and encourage learners to identify further resources.

2. Give learners two to five days to study the course materials (depending on the scope of the content included in the activity).

3. Have learners prepare summaries of their assigned "chunks."

4. Have learners post their summaries to their groups' forums in the asynchronous discussion board.

5. Give each group one to three days to discuss and answer the case-based question(s).

6. Review the summaries provided by the learners to ensure that the materials they are providing to their peers are both adequate and/or accurate.

7. On the last day of the activity, each group should post one report answering the assigned case-based question(s).

Facilitator Notes

- As a variation, allow groups of learners assigned to the same content "chunk" to develop a common summary. Although each learner will still be required to facilitate his or her summary in the assigned cooperative learning group, the common summary can reduce the variation you may have across summaries from one learner group to the next (thus reducing the amount of time required for reviewing the summaries within each cooperative learning group for adequacy and accuracy).

- At the end of the Online Jigsaw Learning activity, you may wish to take the "best" content-related summaries developed by individual learners and make those available to all learners in the courses, giving all learners the opportunity to study the materials that were available to their peers in other cooperative learning groups during the activity.

- You may also want to encourage study groups or cooperative learning groups to use the course's synchronous chat rooms to develop ideas, create summaries, provide additional information, and build online relationships.

71

Rotating Advisory Groups

Activity Summary

Rotating Advisory Groups can be useful practice for gaining informal feedback from learners throughout the duration of an online course. As the facilitator, you can benefit from the specific comments and suggestions for improving the course that an advisory group can share with you and that you may not otherwise hear from individual learners.

Goals

- Learners will provide informal feedback to the facilitator
- Learners will work collaboratively to identify comments and recommendations for improving the learning experience
- The facilitator will receive informal feedback and make any beneficial modifications to the course

Collaborative Learning

Small groups (3 to 5 learners each)

Recommended e-Learning Experience

Learner—Novice
Facilitator—Novice

Mode

Asynchronous

Time Required
Ongoing task throughout the course

Materials
- Facilitator and learner access to an online asynchronous discussion board
- Facilitator and learner access to email

Preparation
1. Form advisory groups of three to five learners each.
2. Assign each advisory group to a period of time during the course (for example, a lesson, a week, a module).
3. Create a single forum in the course's asynchronous discussion board for the Rotating Advisory Groups activity.

Process
1. Email advisory group members when it their time (a lesson, a week, a module) to provide informal feedback.
2. Encourage advisory group members to contact their peers in the course in order to identify feedback that should be brought to your attention.
3. Have advisory group members post any comments or recommendations in the discussion forum (or send it by email if it requires confidentiality). Advisory group feedback may include comments or recommendations regarding the following:
   - Specific assignments or activities
   - Effectiveness of teams or working groups
   - Pace of the course
   - Technological problems

- Reviews prior to examinations
- Confusion on steps or protocols
- Use of etiquette guidelines

4. Post responses to each comment or recommendation to the advisory discussion forum. There should be no "right" or "wrong" advisory comments or recommendations. Most responses should simply thank the advisory group member for his or her input and identify any modifications to the course that may be appropriate.

5. Rotate from week to week, lesson to lesson, or module to module the assigned advisory group, offering all learners in the course the opportunity to provide feedback to the facilitator.

Facilitator Notes

For short courses (fewer than ten days), it is often helpful to identify a single advisory group. In these cases it is important to provide all learners in the course with a list of the advisory group members and their email addresses. Individual feedback from learners would then be provided directly to the advisory group and then posted to the discussion forum if appropriate.

72

Course S.W.O.T.s

Activity Summary

The Strengths, Weaknesses, Opportunities, and Threats (S.W.O.T) analysis is a technique often used by organizations to examine their past, current, and future performance from multiple perspectives. The Course S.W.O.T.s activity utilizes this same technique to provide the facilitator with essential information for ensuring the success of learners in any online course, improving course materials, and making decisions regarding interactive course activities and assignments.

Goals

- Learners will review course materials in responding to the activity
- Learners will assess course experiences for strengths, weaknesses, opportunities, and threats
- Learners will provide feedback to the instructor related to their assigned S.W.O.T. perspective (strengths, weaknesses, opportunities, or threats)

Collaborative Learning

Small groups (4 learners each)

Recommended e-Learning Experience

Learner—Novice
Facilitator—Novice

Mode
Asynchronous

Time Required
30 to 60 minutes (once during a course for each learner)

Materials
- Facilitator and learner access to an online asynchronous discussion board
- Facilitator and learner access to email

Preparation
1. Form collaborative groups of four learners each.
2. Identify times during your course when you would like to receive feedback from learners on the course activities, assignments, structure, materials, resources, and other aspects. You should select the same number of times as the number of groups you formed (that is, if you have five groups, then you would identify five times during the course for the activity).
3. Assign each collaborative group to a time in the course when they will provide S.W.O.T. feedback (for example, Group A due date for S.W.O.T. is March 10, Group B due date for S.W.O.T. is March 30).
4. Create a forum in the course's asynchronous discussion board for the activity.

Process

1. Email learners with the group assignments and the date when their group is to provide S.W.O.T. feedback.

2. Remind collaborative groups in advance of their due date for the group's S.W.O.T. analysis.

3. Have the learners in each collaborative group work together to identify strengths, weaknesses, opportunities, and threats (at least one in each category) to their success in the course. The analysis should include both an assessment of the course activities, assignments, structure, materials, and resources, as well as an appraisal of learner performance, study skills, learning strategies, and collaboration.

4. Have collaborative groups post to the discussion forum their S.W.O.T. analysis for the course up to that point.

5. Respond to each group's S.W.O.T. analysis with appreciation for their feedback and any specific changes you may choose to make to the online course.

Facilitator Notes

- For the Course S.W.O.T.s activity to be effective, as a facilitator you must recognize that no course is "perfect" and that gaining feedback from learners can provide you with valuable insights for improving course materials and your interactions with learners, as well as strategies for aiding learner performance in the course. In addition, you will likely receive some feedback that is irrelevant or negative, but this too can be useful in understanding the perspective of learners in the course and the challenges they are facing.

- Although some feedback you may receive through the Course S.W.O.T.s activity could be negative, you should encourage learners to provide constructive criticism as well as concrete ideas for how to improve course materials, activities, and assignments.

- As a tool for gaining feedback on specific course activities or assignments, you can also use the Course S.W.O.T.s activity only at strategic times during a course. When using this variation of the activity, you can have all learners in the course provide feedback from an assigned perspective (strengths, weaknesses, opportunities, or threats), then rotate their perspectives for each following S.W.O.T. activity, thereby ensuring that learners have the opportunity to provide feedback from a variety of perspectives during a course. For example, the first time five learners may provide strengths feedback, the next time those five learners would provide weaknesses feedback, and the next time opportunities feedback.

73

Quick Polls and Surveys

Activity Summary

Online facilitators can use Quick Polls and Surveys to gain valuable information from learners at strategic times throughout an online course. You can uses polls and surveys to assess learner understanding of topics, potential confusion on complex course concepts, feedback on collaborative group performance, or other information that is of value in facilitating an effective course.

Goals

- Learners will participate in an online poll or survey
- Learners will provide beneficial information to the facilitator
- Learners will view the poll and survey results to self-assess their performance in the course

Collaborative Learning

Large groups (all learners in a course)

Recommended e-Learning Experience

Learner—Novice
Facilitator—Moderate

Mode

Asynchronous

Time Required

30 to 60 minutes each

Materials

- Facilitator and learner access to an online asynchronous discussion board
- Facilitator and learner access to email
- (Optional) Facilitator and learner access to online polling or survey software

Preparation

1. Identify one or more questions that you would like to ask learners in your course. The question(s) can focus on learner understanding of course content, identify potential confusion around complex course concepts, determine whether learners are on pace with the course, assess learner performance in collaborative groups, or ask for additional information that will be useful to you as the facilitator of the course.

2. Create a forum in the course's asynchronous discussion forum for the activity.

Process

1. Email learners with instructions for participating in the Quick Poll or Survey, including a time limit for their response (24 hours, 36 hours).

2. Post the question(s) you have identified for the activity as separate postings to the discussion forum.

3. Have learners respond to the posted question(s).

4. Tally the responses to each question.

5. Post a summary of the responses provided by the participating learners (for example, "25 percent of learners indicated that they could not apply the concepts of Situational Leadership® in their current position within their company").

Facilitator Notes

Specialized online polling or survey software can also be used to facilitate the activity. Many course management systems (such as Blackboard®, WebCT®, and LearningSpace®) include these features, and a variety of independent websites (for example, WebMonkey® and Zoomerang®) offer similar services at little or no cost. Facilitators with advanced technical skills can also create their own online polls or surveys by adding CGI or Java scripts to their webpages.

74

Frequently Asked Questions (FAQs)

Activity Summary

The FAQs activity is a twist on the common practice of websites to provide a list of "Frequently Asked Questions" and the company's responses. In the FAQs activity, however, the facilitator will provide the questions and the learners will provide the answers.

Goals

- Learners will develop the skills of finding answers to questions using online resources
- Learners will provide the answers to a set of frequently asked questions for later use in the course

Collaborative Learning

Large groups (all learners in a course)

Recommended e-Learning Experience

Learner—Novice
Facilitator—Novice

Mode

Asynchronous

Time Required

Approximately two to three days for every ten questions

Materials

- Facilitator and learner access to the World Wide Web
- Facilitator and learner access to an online asynchronous discussion board

Preparation

1. Identify ten to twenty questions that are frequently asked by learners in the course (if this is your first time teaching the course, then you may want to use general questions learners may ask about course assignments, available technical support, using online databases, etc.).
2. Create a forum in the course's asynchronous discussion board for the activity.
3. Post the FAQs that you have identified to the discussion forum.

Process

1. Have learners post answers to the FAQs included in the discussion forum. All answers must include a reference that can be used to verify the information (a webpage, a text, the course syllabus).
2. Post a message ending the discussion thread for individual questions when you believe that a question is adequately answered.
3. Collect the "best" answers at the end of the activity and include all of those in a single posting to the discussion area that learners will be able to refer back to throughout the remainder of the course.

Facilitator Notes

Learners may also be asked to contribute questions that would be useful to have in a FAQs knowledge base for the remainder of the course. Learners can then post questions that their peers will answer as part of the activity.

75

Quick Quizzes

Activity Summary

Like the familiar "shot gun" classroom game where facilitators ask a series of questions and the first learner to respond gets a point, the Quick Quizzes activity transforms this approach for online courses by using a synchronous chat room. As a technique for reviewing course materials or preparing learners for an end-of-course exam, Quick Quizzes can be used to engage learners and offer them an opportunity to interact online with their peers.

Goals

- Learners will review course materials in answering questions
- Learners will interact with their peers in a synchronous online chat room

Collaborative Learning

Large groups (all learners in a course)

Recommended e-Learning Experience

Learner—Novice
Facilitator—Novice

Mode

Synchronous

Time Required

40 to 60 minutes

Materials

Facilitator and learner access to a synchronous chat room

Preparation

1. Identify a synchronous chat room for the activity. Most online course delivery tools (Blackboard®, WebCT®, Learning-Space®) offer multiple chat rooms that can be used simultaneously for group activities or alone for whole-class activities. From the available chat rooms, select a specific chat room (chat room one or chat room A) for the activity.

2. Establish a date and time when the most learners from the course will be available to participate in a synchronous chat room discussion. Depending on the location and schedules of learners, it may be necessary to plan for two or more Quick Quizzes.

3. Create a list of twenty to thirty quick-response questions based on course materials (short answer, true/false, yes/no). Have the questions saved in a word processing file so you can cut and paste them into the chat quickly.

Process

1. Cut and paste your first question into the chat room.

2. Have learners post their answers to the question in the chat room.

3. Indicate when a learner has posted the correct answer (for example,, "That is correct, Rachelle").

4. Write down the names of the learners who correctly answered the question on a piece of paper.

5. Cut and paste your second question into the chat room, and the follow the same steps until you have asked all of your questions.

6. Identify the learner who answered the most questions correctly.

Facilitator Notes

As an alternative to identifying the quick questions for the activity yourself, you can ask learners to submit potential questions prior to the activity. This will assist you in building a comprehensive list of questions as well as give individual learners the advantage of being able to quickly answer their own question and gain points.

Glossary*

....

Asynchronous. Discussions that do not necessarily take place at the same time (such as those on email or discussion boards).

Attachment. A file that is coupled to an email or other Internet communication.

Chat. To communicate on the Internet in real-time (i.e., synchronous communications).

Discussion board. An asynchronous online communications tool that allows users to leave messages, review messages, and upload/download attachments (also commonly called an online bulletin board system or BBS).

Email. An asynchronous online communications tool for sending messages from one computer to another.

Emoticons. A combination of characters used in online communications to represent a human emotion or attitudes: for example, happiness with: -), laughter with: -D, or sadness with: -(.

Forums. Sections created within a discussion board where distinct topics can be discussed.

Homepage. The first screen containing information that you see when you arrive at a website.

Instant messenger. A synchronous online communications tool that allows users to have real-time chats with other users without relying on a third-party computer to host the chat.

*Based on Watkins and Corry, 2005, and Kleinedler, 2001.

Listserv. A list used to distribute emails among the group's members.

Online survey or poll. Web-based software that allows users to create and/or respond to survey questions using the World Wide Web; most also include options that allow users to view the resulting aggregated data from the survey or poll immediately after responding.

Plug-in. Software applications that can be added to a Web browser to expand its capabilities (for example, Macromedia Flash® or Macintosh QuickTime® for playing animations).

Real-time chat. To communicate on the Internet in real-time (synchronous communications).

Search engine. A program that searches for websites and other information on the World Wide Web.

Synchronous. Communications that take place at the same time (such as real-time chat or instant messenger).

Thread. A series of messages that have been posted on an online discussion board that typically include visual indicators to illustrate which messages are replies to other messages.

URL. The Uniform Resource Locator (or URL) is the address used to locate information available on the World Wide Web. For example, http://www.gwu.edu or http://www.pfeiffer.com.

Web browser. A software application, such as Microsoft Internet Explorer® or Netscape Navigator®, that allows you to find and access documents available on the World Wide Web.

Webliography. A bibliography of World Wide Web resources.

Webpage. A file on the World Wide Web that is accessible using a Web browser.

Website. A set of interconnected webpages.

References

Conner, M. (2004). *Learn more now*. Hoboken, NJ: John Wiley & Sons. Retrieved on January 25, 2004, from http://agelesslearner.com/assess/learningstyle.html

de Bono, E. (1994). *de Bono's thinking course* (3rd ed.). New York: Facts On File.

Fulwiler, T. (2004, February). Writing in the disciplines (workshop). Washington, DC: The George Washington University.

Group effectiveness: Understanding group member roles. (1994, October 1). East Lansing, MI: Michigan State University Extension. Retrieved January 19, 2004, from www.msue.msu.edu/msue/imp/modii/ii719202.html

Johnson, D.W., & Johnson, R.T. (1992). Encouraging thinking through constructive controversy. In N. Davidson & T. Worsham (Eds.), *Enhancing thinking through cooperative learning* (pp. 120–137). New York: Teachers College Press.

Kleinedler, S. (Ed.). (2001). *Dictionary of computer and internet words: An a to z guide to hardware, software, and cyberspace*. New York: Houghton Mifflin.

Ko, S., & Rossen, S. (2004). *Teaching online: A practical guide* (2nd ed.). New York: Houghton Mifflin.

Koppett, K., & Richter, M. (2001). How to use storytelling to increase learning. In *Setting norms for collaborative work*. Boston, MA: Center for Collaborative Education. Retrieved January 19, 2004, from www.turningpts.org/pdf/SettingNorms.pdf

Tuckman, B. (1965). Development sequence in small groups. *Psychological Bulletin, 63*(6).

Watkins, R., & Corry, M. (2005). *e-Learning companion: A student's guide to online success*. New York: Houghton Mifflin.

Additional Resources

Dick, W., Carey, L., & Carey, J. (2001). *The systematic design of instruction* (5th ed.). New York: Addison Wesley Longman.

Graham, C.R. (2002). *Understanding and facilitating computer-mediated teamwork: A study of how norms develop in online learning teams.* Doctoral dissertation, Indiana University, Bloomington, IN. Retrieved February 19, 2004, from www.byu.edu/ipt/faculty/displayfacultypage.php?nav=graham

Kagan, S. (1992). *Cooperative learning.* San Juan Capistrano, CA: P. Kagan Cooperative Learning.

Silberman, M. (Ed.). (2001). *The 2001 training and performance sourcebook.* New York: McGraw-Hill. Retrieved February 2, 2004, from www.thestorynet. com/articles_essays/storyuse.htm

Silberman, M., & Lawson, K. (1995). *101 ways to make training activity.* San Francisco, CA: Pfeiffer.

Sugar, S., & Takacs, G. (2004). *Games that teach teams: 21 activities to super-charge your group!* San Francisco, CA: Pfeiffer.

Sugar, S., & Willet, C. (2004). *Games that boost performance.* San Francisco, CA: Pfeiffer.

Thiagarajan, S. (2003). *Design your own games and activities: Thiagi's templates for performance improvement.* San Francisco, CA: Pfeiffer.

Index

About the Author

RYAN WATKINS is an associate professor of educational technology at The George Washington University in Washington, D.C. He received his doctoral degree from Florida State University in instructional systems design, and he has additional formal training in Web design, change management, and program evaluation. Ryan designs and teaches course in instructional design, distance education, needs assessment, system analysis and design, research methods, and technology management for both online and classroom delivery. Previously, he was a professor of instructional technology and distance education at Nova Southeastern University. He was also a member of the research faculty in the Learning Systems Institute at Florida State University.

He is an author of three books, including the best-selling *e-Learning Companion: A Student's Guide to Online Success* (Houghton Mifflin, 2005) and *Strategic Planning for Success: Aligning People, Performance, and Payoffs* (Pfeiffer, 2003). He has also published more than fifty articles on the topics of strategic planning, distance education, needs assessment, return-on-investment analysis, and evaluation. He is an active member of the International Society for Performance Improvement (ISPI) and the United States Distance Learning Association, and he has served as vice president of the Inter-American Distance Education Consortium (CREAD).

Ryan offers a variety of e-learning workshops and consulting services on topics including instructional design, interactive e-learning activities, and preparing learners for online success. For more information contact him at rwatkins@gwu.edu or visit www.ryanrwatkins.com.

How to Use the CD-ROM

System Requirements

Windows PC

- 486 or Pentium processor-based personal computer
- Microsoft Windows 95 or Windows NT 3.51 or later
- Minimum RAM: 8MB for Windows 95 and NT
- Available space on hard disk: 8 MB Windows 95 and NT
- 2X speed CD-ROM drive or faster

Macintosh

- Macintosh with a 68020 or higher processor or Power Macintosh
- Apple OS version 7.0 or later
- Minimum RAM: 12MB for Macintosh
- Available space on hard disk: 6MB Macintosh
- 2X speed CD-ROM drive or faster

NOTE: This CD requires Netscape 3.0 or MS Internet Explorer 3.0 or higher. You can download these products using the links on the CD-ROM Help Page.

Getting Started

Insert the CD-ROM into your drive. The CD-ROM will usually launch automatically. If it does not, click on the CD-ROM drive on your computer to launch. After you click to agree to the terms of the Copyright Page, the Home Page will appear.

Moving Around

Use the buttons at the left of each screen to move among the menu pages. To view a document listed on one of the menu pages, simply click on the name of the document. To quit a document at any time, click the box at the upper right-hand corner of the screen.

To quit the CD-ROM, you can click the Exit button or hit Alt-F4.

To Download Documents

Open the document you wish to download. Under the File pull-down menu, choose Save As. Save the document onto your hard drive with a different name. It is important to use a different name, otherwise the document may remain a read-only file.

You can also click on your CD drive in Windows Explorer and select a document to copy it to your hard drive and rename it.

In Case of Trouble

If you experience difficulty using this CD-ROM, please follow these steps:

1. Make sure your hardware and systems configurations conform to the systems requirements noted under "Systems Requirements" above.

2. Review the installation procedure for your type of hardware and operating system. It is possible to reinstall the software if necessary.

3. Have a question, comment, or suggestion? Contact us! We value your feedback, and we want to hear from you.

For questions about this or other Pfeiffer products, you may contact us by:

E-mail: customer@wiley.com
Mail: Customer Care Wiley/Pfeiffer
         10475 Crosspoint Blvd.
         Indianapolis, IN 46256
Phone: (U.S.) 800–274–4434 (Outside the U.S. 317–572–3985)
Fax: (U.S.) 800–569–0443 (Outside the U.S. 317–572–4002)

To order additional copies of this product or to browse other Pfeiffer products visit us online at www.pfeiffer.com.

To speak with someone in Product Technical Support, call 800–762–2974 or 317–572–3994 Monday through Friday 8:30 a.m. to 5 p.m. (EST). You can also contact Product Technical Support and get support information through our website at http://www.wiley.com/techsupport

Before calling or writing, please have the following information available:

- Type of operating system
- Any error messages displayed
- Complete description of the problem

It is best if you are sitting at your computer when making the call.

Pfeiffer Publications Guide

This guide is designed to familiarize you with the various types of Pfeiffer publications. The formats section describes the various types of products that we publish; the methodologies section describes the many different ways that content might be provided within a product. We also provide a list of the topic areas in which we publish.

FORMATS

In addition to its extensive book-publishing program, Pfeiffer offers content in an array of formats, from fieldbooks for the practitioner to complete, ready-to-use training packages that support group learning.

FIELDBOOK Designed to provide information and guidance to practitioners in the midst of action. Most fieldbooks are companions to another, sometimes earlier, work, from which its ideas are derived; the fieldbook makes practical what was theoretical in the original text. Fieldbooks can certainly be read from cover to cover. More likely, though, you'll find yourself bouncing around following a particular theme, or dipping in as the mood, and the situation, dictate.

HANDBOOK A contributed volume of work on a single topic, comprising an eclectic mix of ideas, case studies, and best practices sourced by practitioners and experts in the field.

An editor or team of editors usually is appointed to seek out contributors and to evaluate content for relevance to the topic. Think of a handbook not as a ready-to-eat meal, but as a cookbook of ingredients that enables you to create the most fitting experience for the occasion.

RESOURCE Materials designed to support group learning. They come in many forms: a complete, ready-to-use exercise (such as a game); a comprehensive resource on one topic (such as conflict management) containing a variety of methods and approaches; or a collection of like-minded activities (such as icebreakers) on multiple subjects and situations.

TRAINING PACKAGE An entire, ready-to-use learning program that focuses on a particular topic or skill. All packages comprise a guide for the facilitator/trainer and a workbook for the participants. Some packages are supported with additional media—such as video—or learning aids, instruments, or other devices to help participants understand concepts or practice and develop skills.

- *Facilitator/trainer's guide* Contains an introduction to the program, advice on how to organize and facilitate the learning event, and step-by-step instructor notes. The guide also contains copies of presentation materials—handouts, presentations, and overhead designs, for example—used in the program.

- *Participant's workbook* Contains exercises and reading materials that support the learning goal and serves as a valuable reference and support guide for participants in the weeks and months that follow the learning event. Typically, each participant will require his or her own workbook.

ELECTRONIC CD-ROMs and web-based products transform static Pfeiffer content into dynamic, interactive experiences. Designed to take advantage of the searchability, automation, and ease-of-use that technology provides, our e-products bring convenience and immediate accessibility to your workspace.

METHODOLOGIES

CASE STUDY A presentation, in narrative form, of an actual event that has occurred inside an organization. Case studies are not prescriptive, nor are they used to prove a point; they are designed to develop critical analysis and decision-making skills. A case study has a specific time frame, specifies a sequence of events, is narrative in structure, and contains a plot structure—an issue (what should be/have been done?). Use case studies when the goal is to enable participants to apply previously learned theories to the circumstances in the case, decide what is pertinent, identify the real issues, decide what should have been done, and develop a plan of action.

ENERGIZER A short activity that develops readiness for the next session or learning event. Energizers are most commonly used after a break or lunch to stimulate or refocus the group. Many involve some form of physical activity, so they are a useful way to counter post-lunch lethargy. Other uses include transitioning from one topic to another, where "mental" distancing is important.

EXPERIENTIAL LEARNING ACTIVITY (ELA) A facilitator-led intervention that moves participants through the learning cycle from experience to application (also known as a Structured Experience). ELAs are carefully thought-out designs in which there is a definite learning purpose and intended outcome. Each step—everything that participants do during the activity—facilitates the accomplishment of the stated goal. Each ELA includes complete instructions for facilitating the intervention and a clear statement of goals, suggested group size and timing, materials required, an explanation of the process, and, where appropriate, possible variations to the activity. (For more detail on Experiential Learning Activities, see the Introduction to the *Reference Guide to Handbooks and Annuals*, 1999 edition, Pfeiffer, San Francisco.)

GAME A group activity that has the purpose of fostering team spirit and togetherness in addition to the achievement of a pre-stated goal. Usually contrived—undertaking a desert expedition, for example—this type of learning method offers an engaging means for participants to demonstrate and practice business and interpersonal skills. Games are effective for team building and personal development mainly because the goal is subordinate to the process—the means through which participants reach decisions, collaborate, communicate, and generate trust and understanding. Games often engage teams in "friendly" competition.

ICEBREAKER A (usually) short activity designed to help participants overcome initial anxiety in a training session and/or to acquaint the participants with one another. An icebreaker can be a fun activity or can be tied to specific topics or training goals. While a useful tool in itself, the icebreaker comes into its own in situations where tension or resistance exists within a group.

INSTRUMENT A device used to assess, appraise, evaluate, describe, classify, and summarize various aspects of human behavior. The term used to describe an instrument depends primarily on its format and purpose. These terms include survey, questionnaire, inventory, diagnostic, survey, and poll. Some uses of instruments include providing instrumental feedback to group members, studying here-and-now processes or functioning within a group, manipulating group composition, and evaluating outcomes of training and other interventions.

Instruments are popular in the training and HR field because, in general, more growth can occur if an individual is provided with a method for focusing specifically on his or her own behavior. Instruments also are used to obtain information that will serve as a basis for change and to assist in workforce planning efforts.

Paper-and-pencil tests still dominate the instrument landscape with a typical package comprising a facilitator's guide, which offers advice on administering the instrument and interpreting the collected data, and an initial set of instruments. Additional instruments are available separately. Pfeiffer, though, is investing heavily in e-instruments. Electronic instrumentation provides effortless distribution and, for larger groups particularly, offers advantages over paper-and-pencil tests in the time it takes to analyze data and provide feedback.

LECTURETTE A short talk that provides an explanation of a principle, model, or process that is pertinent to the participants' current learning needs. A lecturette is intended to establish a common language bond between the trainer and the participants by providing a mutual frame of reference. Use a lecturette as an introduction to a group activity or event, as an interjection during an event, or as a handout.

MODEL A graphic depiction of a system or process and the relationship among its elements. Models provide a frame of reference and something more tangible, and more easily remembered, than a verbal explanation. They also give participants something to "go on," enabling them to track their own progress as they experience the dynamics, processes, and relationships being depicted in the model.

ROLE PLAY A technique in which people assume a role in a situation/scenario: a customer service rep in an angry-customer exchange, for example. The way in which the role is approached is then discussed and feedback is offered. The role play is often repeated using a different approach and/or incorporating changes made based on feedback received. In other words, role playing is a spontaneous interaction involving realistic behavior under artificial (and safe) conditions.

SIMULATION A methodology for understanding the interrelationships among components of a system or process. Simulations differ from games in that they test or use a model that depicts or mirrors some aspect of reality in form, if not necessarily in content. Learning occurs by studying the effects of change on one or more factors of the model. Simulations are commonly used to test hypotheses about what happens in a system—often referred to as "what if?" analysis—or to examine best-case/worst-case scenarios.

THEORY A presentation of an idea from a conjectural perspective. Theories are useful because they encourage us to examine behavior and phenomena through a different lens.

TOPICS

The twin goals of providing effective and practical solutions for workforce training and organization development and meeting the educational needs of training and human resource professionals shape Pfeiffer's publishing program. Core topics include the following:

Leadership & Management

Communication & Presentation

Coaching & Mentoring

Training & Development

e-Learning

Teams & Collaboration

OD & Strategic Planning

Human Resources

Consulting